GEORGE ELBERT BURR

Catalogue Raisonné and Guide to the Etched Works

GEORGE ELBERT BURR

1859–1939

Catalogue Raisonné and Guide to the Etched Works

with Biographical and Critical Notes

LOUISE COMBES SEEBER

NORTHLAND PRESS / FLAGSTAFF, ARIZONA / 1971

ISBN NUMBER 0-87358-067-2

LIBRARY OF CONGRESS CATALOG NUMBER 78-150685

Contents

List of Illustrations

*The pastel and watercolor, and except as noted otherwise, the etchings
and photographs are from the author's personal collection*

Preface

IN 1809 SYLVESTER GAYLORD was brought by his parents to the Connecticut Western Reserve, where he lived his entire life in a place now known as Munroe Falls, Ohio. He had five children by his second wife; his eldest daughter, Lucy, was George Elbert Burr's mother, and his youngest, Julia (Mrs. Willard Wright Wetmore), was my maternal grandmother. After the Burrs moved in 1869 to Cameron, Missouri, when George Elbert was only ten years old, the Gaylords, a large and closely knit group, remained for many years in Munroe Falls and in near-by Stow Corners. But Cousin Bert was to see little of them during the succeeding years, and after his marriage in 1884 he visited his Ohio relatives only once (without Betty, his wife), a few months before I was born.

Our ties with him were none the less deep-rooted, and despite various obstacles to personal contacts — his unceasing and demanding work, the many miles that had always separated us, and his wife's untoward possessiveness[1] — his name was a household word in our family; we received frequent assurances of his affection, and kept in touch with his distinguished career through letters from Betty Burr (which,

---

[1] Cousin Bert's much younger brother Linn (a farmer and veterinarian in Cameron) and his wife Eva were frequent guests in the Burrs' home; but Betty Burr, after her return from Europe, made it abundantly clear that her husband's relatives on his mother's side — indeed, even his parents and sister Bessie — were not welcome there, and when the artist died she sent no notice to our family until after the funeral. However regrettable her behavior, we accepted it dispassionately. We knew that she lived for her husband as he lived for his art; we always spoke of them as one, "Cousin Bert-and-Betty."

paradoxically enough, were cordial and full of concern for the "dear ones") and by long and pleasant reunions with his mother and sister Bessie, who would come from Cameron to stay at the Wetmore home in Stow Corners. In this house I was born and, as a child, spent my first sixteen summers and countless weekends. Many unforgettable circumstances during these early years brought the name of my kinsman constantly to mind — his one-man show of watercolors in Cleveland to which I, not yet of kindergarten age, was dutifully taken by my proud mother; my discovery of the carefully preserved studio in the attic of the Gaylord homestead in Munroe Falls where my "illustrious cousin" (as my great-aunt Mary Brewster Gaylord commonly referred to him) had been taught by his mother to draw and paint as a boy of six; the familiar paintings and etchings in my grandmother's house (frequent gifts from her nephew) and in our Cleveland home.

In the course of time I acquired some Burr etchings of my own, and by the end of 1961, their number having substantially increased, I began to study a few notable collections and to examine the rather sparse literature pertaining to the artist and his work. I was immediately struck by the need for a definitive treatise in this field; I found, for example, that the two existing *catalogues raisonnés*, published in 1923 and 1930, were incomplete and, in many respects, inaccurate; that a number of Burr etchings in collections or published as reproductions had been incorrectly identified and mistitled owing to subtle complexities to which the artist himself sometimes unwittingly contributed; and that biographical sources contained persistent misstatements of fact and regrettable omissions. Two years later, with the encouragement of Henry P. Rossiter, then Curator of Prints and Drawings in the Boston Museum of Fine Arts, I resolved to prepare a precise list and description of Burr's etchings that would provide dimensions and etching processes employed, alternate titles, a clear differentiation of etchings that bear identical or similar titles, and other data indispensable for positive identification and correct cataloguing, together with appropriate facts about the artist's life and career.

My project would not have been feasible without the opportunity to study, in addition to etchings of my own, important collections in the New York Public Library, Metropolitan Museum of Art, Library of Congress, Denver Public Library, Phoenix Art Museum, Arizona State University, Fogg Art Museum, Boston Museum of Fine Arts, and British Museum. I profited also from visits to collections in the Cincinnati Art Museum, Grand Rapids Art Gallery, Oklahoma Art Center in Oklahoma City, Nelson Gallery of Art in Kansas City, Missouri, and elsewhere.

I was pleased at the outset to find that my appreciation of the etchings was greatly enhanced by my first-hand knowledge of the subjects depicted in many of them, for I was no stranger to the Arizona desert, the Apache Trail, and the Grand Canyon; I had camped more than once near the Spanish Peaks and along the Front Range of the Rockies, climbed Longs Peak and Hallett Peak, hiked around Bear Lake and Bear Creek Canyon, and visited Switzerland and the Italian lakes. During later sojourns abroad with our car, as I unhurriedly followed Burr's itinerary through Italy to Sicily, through Switzerland to the Rhine castles and German cities, then to London, Oxford, and North Wales, I continued to gain a more precise understanding of the etchings and useful material for pertinent commentaries — for example, through the discovery of the exact scene shown in #55 *Street in Sierre, Suisse*, which has often been mistitled *Street in Sion, Switzerland.*

Many persons have helped me most generously in my search for information and documents relating to Burr, and for examples of his work. I am especially indebted to Mrs. Katharine D. Barnes and Mrs. Alys Freeze of the Denver Public Library; Miss Ruth E. Dickey of the Indiana State Library, Indianapolis; Mr. William Duprey, formerly of the New York Public Library; Mrs. Ruth R. Harlow of the Connecticut Historical Society, Hartford; Mrs. Fritz Hart of the Honolulu Academy of Arts; Mrs. Lorena Jones of the *Denver Post* library; Mr. R. D. A. Puckle and Mrs. Norma King of the Phoenix Art Museum; Miss Ruth Magurn of the Fogg Art Museum; Mrs. Marion Murra, Reference Librarian, Pueblo Regional Library; Professor Robert M. Ormes of Colorado College; Miss Helen Perniece of the Cincinnati Art Museum; Mr. Henry P. Rossiter, formerly of the Boston Museum of Fine Arts; Miss Elizabeth Roth of the New York Public Library; Dr. Julia Sabine of the Public Library, Newark, N.J.; and Mr. Carl Zigrosser, formerly of the Philadelphia Museum of Art. For their many services and courtesies I am grateful also to the staffs of the Boston Public Library, California Palace of the Legion of Honor, California State Library, Library of Congress, Santa Barbara Public Library, Smithsonian Institution, Stow (Ohio) Public Library, and numerous historical societies and archives in Ohio, Missouri, Colorado, Arizona, and California.

I owe much to the late Frank A. Green of Stow, Ohio, a lifelong friend with whom I am proud to claim kinship (we were both related to Abiah Gaylord, mother of Leonard Case, Jr., founder of Case School of Applied Science in Cleveland). During the last five years of his life (he died in 1968 less than a month before his one-hundredth birthday) he provided me, both in person and in long, detailed letters, with invaluable information about local history; his sage advice and lively interest in my work are gratefully remembered. The late Lawrence Spore, who as a boy in Cameron was well acquainted with the Burr family, also supplied me with important material in a correspondence that continued for more than two years.

In her readiness to share with me her recollections of the Burr family, Mrs. R. F. Goodman, of Cameron, has been singularly obliging and helpful. Her continuing interest in my project, and generous gifts of the Burr family Bible and other precious items, have on more than one occasion brought me pleasure and encouragement.

Very special thanks go to our daughter Betty for her able and willing management of the household while this volume was in progress, and to my husband, Edward D. Seeber, for his companionship during my travels, his constant sharing of my problems and successes, and his unsparing assistance in the preparation of my manuscript.

Technical terms used are explained in the Glossary following the Appendix.

L.C.S.

Bloomington, Indiana

George Elbert Burr   The Etcher

#300   *The Etcher*   7 x 5 inches.

Burr at his geared press, a self-portrait

1

Introduction

WHEN GEORGE ELBERT BURR was six years old he was already enjoying daily instruction, from his mother, in drawing and painting. By the close of his career, at the age of eighty, he had made good in important assignments as a magazine and book illustrator, produced pencil, wash, and silver-point drawings, a few lithographs, some fifty oils, over a thousand watercolors, and two thousand pen-and-ink drawings. His crowning achievement, over a period of nearly seventy years, was the pulling of some twenty-five thousand etchings on his own presses.[1] In large measure he owed this prolificacy —which was the more remarkable in a man who often suffered from periods of poor health and near exhaustion — to his unremitting travels in pursuit of natural beauty, his complete devotion to the creative work that he loved and in which he firmly believed, and a perseverance that showed him to be a man, as Sir Joshua Reynolds said of Michelangelo, "distinguished even from his infancy for his indefatigable diligence; and this was continued through his whole life. . . ."[2]

Various records of Burr's personal contacts reveal his intimate

---

[1] This is a conservative estimate. In 1927 — only three years after moving to Phoenix — Burr wrote to the Denver dealer Cyrus Boutwell: "[I] have made 286 plates and printed 11,168 etchings, not counting the little Christmas cards which number 9,300 — a total of 20,468. No wonder I am tired!" (Quoted from the A. Reynolds Morse manuscript "The Life and Works of George Elbert Burr" now owned by the Denver Public Library.) During the twelve years that followed, Burr made many of his most successful etchings, some in editions of 200. His estimates of the number of oils, watercolors, and black-and-white drawings are from another letter to Boutwell (Aug. 16, 1932) as reported by Morse.

[2] Fifteenth Discourse to members of the Royal Academy, Dec. 10, 1790.

thoughts about his craft and about his life as an artist. Ten years prior to his death he confided to Leila Mechlin, secretary of the American Federation of Arts, that his two greatest pleasures in life were "the joy of doing my work," and "learning that it gives pleasure to others."[3] In a letter of January 9, 1930, he confessed to R. P. Tolman, assistant curator in the Division of Graphic Arts at the Smithsonian Institution: "It's lots of fun to be a 'poor artist.' Nearly fifty years I've been, except for health limitations, supremely happy in my work, and am constantly surprised in the number of people that also seem to get pleasure out of my labor. It all seems so odd, that without effort, I've always sold more than Mrs. Burr and I have needed for all our fourteen years of travel and other so-called luxuries." He continued to dwell on these bounteous years in another letter to Leila Mechlin, dated March 5, 1934: "As long as I can work a little, for the pure joy of it, Mrs. B. and I are happy — in fact we have had fifty years of an 'Alice in Wonderland' journey through life. The world has been so kind, I've done just what I enjoyed doing, and never a worry, as the world always gives us more money than we need." In precisely the same vein he wrote on April 3, 1936, to Frank Weitenkampf, then Curator of Prints at the New York Public Library: "Mrs. Burr and I have had so much happiness, done almost everything we ever wanted to do, and have no worries of any kind."

Burr was essentially a simple, dedicated, high-principled man who employed his talents, in the words of Arthur Millier, art editor of the *Los Angeles Times* and himself an etcher, "not to please fashion or make money, but to interpret the things that stirred him the most deeply."[4] His modesty and staunch independence were exemplary. By nature he was not aggressive, and showed no inclination to seek either publicity, popularity, or honors — even, as Millier remarks, prizes at exhibitions; and although his profession alone supplied his livelihood, "art for him was not commercial. If anything was commercial or useful it was not art. None of his etchings were begun or thought of as for sale."[5] He did, in fact, in order to discourage inflated prices, steadfastly refuse to grant exclusive dealerships, although during exhibitions or through ordinary avenues of distribution his works were offered for sale at many galleries in major cities. And the market was never slack: he wrote on November 10, 1926, to the Macbeth Gallery in New York: "I should like very much to have someone in New York City push my work, but as I have sold all I could produce in past years, have made no effort to do so." It is much to his credit that, having

3 "New Plates by George Elbert Burr," *The American Magazine of Art,* XX (June 1929), 333.

4 Introduction to *George Elbert Burr,* American Etchers series, Vol. VII (New York & London, [1930]), p. [5].

5 Personal letter of Aug. 28, 1966, from Carl Zigrosser, who became Curator of Prints, Drawings, and Illustrated Books at the Philadelphia Museum of Art shortly after visiting Burr in Phoenix during the summer of 1939.

FIGURE 1a — Simeon North flintlock pistol, model 1819.

North (1765–1852), Burr's great-great-grand-father and the author's great-great-great-grand-father, signed his first Government contract to supply large-caliber pistols (which he designed) in 1799 at the age of thirty-four. The hinged ramrod was an improvement in the model shown. *In the author's collection*

FIGURE 1b — Sèvres porcelain painted by Burr's mother. *In the author's collection*

FIGURE 2 — Wash drawing of Stow Pond (Silver Lake), Ohio.

India ink. 5¾ x 9⅞ inches. Made at about age ten and presented to his aunt Julia Gaylord, who became Mrs. Willard W. Wetmore, the author's grandmother.

In 1874 Ralph Lodge, uncle of the author's father, bought the adjoining property to the north and west, planted 1,000 maple trees, built an island, renamed the lake, and developed one of the finest amusement parks in northern Ohio. Silver Lake is now an attractive residential area.

3

discovered that ownership of his works afforded immense enjoyment, he offered them at prices that individuals and institutions alike could well afford.[6] This mark of consideration further vindicated his credo expressed during the last summer of his life, at the time of Mr. Zigrosser's visit: "If you stick to what you want to do, you will succeed." A note published seven years earlier stated that he was then "probably more numerously represented in the museums of the world than any other living artist of the graphic medium."[7]

One may suppose that many who visited Burr's Phoenix studio in the late thirties did not realize that this active man had been born prior to the Civil War during the presidency of James Buchanan, and that his first attempts at etching had already been made by the early 1870s. Etching, at that date, had made little headway in the United States; the first society of etchers, in New York City, would not be founded until 1877, and Millier related that around 1902, when Burr paid occasional visits to Keppel's, in that city, the firm "was practically alone in the print-dealing field."[8] But in England a revival of the venerable craft was in full flower under master craftsmen like the two expatriates Alphonse Legros and James McNeill Whistler, and, especially, the latter's brother-in-law Sir Francis Seymour Haden, and these continued to work and to carry their prestige into the early 1900s. Also influential was the ill-fated and engrossing French etcher Charles Méryon, who had died in 1868.

That Burr found the work of this older generation congenial is suggested by the degree in which his own paintings and etchings reflect, both in subject matter and technique, the vogue, at the turn of the century, of landscapes and studies of architecture. It is more than likely that he respected the work of Haden, most of which was done before 1880. He was forty-one years Burr's senior, a connoisseur of Rembrandt's etchings, and a great believer in soundness of style; his two stimulating lecture tours in the United States, when Burr was

---

[6] In 1914 the average price of forty-nine of his black-and-white etchings listed in Smalley's catalogue (McPherson, Kan.) was $7.55. Ten color etchings were priced at $10 each, three at $15. Sixteen titles in the first group, averaging $11.06 each, were offered in 1925 by Miller-Sterling Co. (Phoenix) at an average of $22.75. In 1921 the average cost of a single etching in the distinguished Desert Set was only $18.75.

When Burr died intestate, his widow, under community property law, became his sole heir, disposed of a certain number of finished etchings (according to a letter to my parents) and sold the remainder to "four dealers, three here [in Phoenix] and one in Denver . . . at the same price as Bert did. That helps to keep the price within reach of moderate incomes even in the East and Middle West."

[7] "26 Museums Own 700 Works by Burr, Etcher," *Art Digest*, VI (June 1932), 16. While Burr was alive, this figure was raised to 900, and today the number available to the public is even greater if one includes universities, public libraries, and art galleries. Numerous private collections, too, have been assembled since Burr's death. An early pamphlet prepared by the dealer Boutwell stated that collections of Burr's etchings could be found in ten countries. Some of these, notably that in the former Luxembourg Museum in Paris, have since been dispersed or become less accessible for other reasons.

[8] Article in the *Los Angeles Times*, c. 1930; cited from a nine-page brochure of reprinted press clippings, published in Phoenix.

a young man, were long remembered. A review in the *New York Commercial Advertiser* on the occasion of an early exhibition of Burr's watercolors that traveled through the East around 1905 (this was before he moved to Denver to enter upon the most productive period of his long career) commented that viewers "familiar with many of the scenes . . . will find refreshing souvenirs of their visit," and that the same compositions would appeal to the "casual spectator . . . with scarcely less force, for they are honest endeavors to recall the place and the hour."[9] This frankly representational treatment of engaging themes that is found both in his paintings and etchings can, of course, straightway be labeled "traditional."

But if this term is used to define Burr's position as an artist, it must be qualified in the light of his ideals and accomplishments. Broadly speaking it would be correct to say, not that he imitated the etchers of the day, but that he strove continually to improve upon them and to attain perfection as he himself saw it. Several important advantages helped him achieve this aim: he was an ardent student of nature and a competent horticulturist (see Chapter II under years 1876, 1901); he was an accomplished painter (which most etchers of his time were not); he enjoyed the independence of an artist who was self-taught,[10] whose taste and individual style had been shaped as a child,[11] and who would always preserve the integrity of his convictions; and he chose, in the Rocky Mountains and the Southwest, fresh and challenging subjects for his major work. Arthur Millier observed in appreciation of Burr that "American etching, with a few exceptions, follows the European traditions of the craft. . . . But we discover few [etchers] who are entirely their own men in both subject material and style";[12] and Will Simmons of Connecticut, a noted etcher and author, found in the thirty-five etchings of Burr's Desert Set "an American point of view, an essentially American theme and combined with these a real Yankee gift of handicraftsmanship."[13]

---

[9] From an undated pamphlet containing reprints of contemporary reviews (see Appendix, n. 1).

[10] Except for the guidance in drawing and painting provided by his mother, and his brief attendance (for three months early in 1879) at the Chicago Academy of Design. *Who's Who in America* and *Who's Who in American Art* stated that Burr "studied five years in France and Italy," a notion that has been repeated by James Laver and others. The statement is at best ambiguous: he did, indeed, as he traveled leisurely from Sicily to North Wales, study the divers prospects and moods of nature and landscape, and his own technique in representing them; but it is not easy to believe that he had either the time or the inclination to seek formal guidance from other artists.

[11] For example, I have in my possession a wash drawing of Silver Lake (then Stow Pond) that he made at about the age of ten (see Fig. 2), showing the same unmistakable feeling for trees, clouds, and sunlight that lends such pleasing qualities to his later work.

[12] *George Elbert Burr*, p. [1]. One recalls that it was a common practice, not only of American painters, but of etchers as well (Whistler, Joseph Pennell, Frank W. Benson, and many others) to live and work abroad.

[13] "George Elbert Burr, Etcher of the American Desert," *The Print Connoisseur*, X (Oct. 1930), 257.

There is a passage in the discourse of Sir Joshua Reynolds already cited that serves as a fitting point of departure in reviewing some of the more particular aspects of Burr's work. "To distinguish between the correctness of drawing," said Reynolds, "and that part which respects the imagination, we may say that the one approaches to the mechanical (which in its way too may make just pretensions to genius), and the other to the poetical." Burr's gift of superb craftsmanship, the "infinite accuracy and minute delicacy"[14] that are so striking in his etchings and that enhance the charm of his watercolors, was rewarded very early in his career, for in 1888, while still living in Missouri, he was doing illustrations for both Scribner's and Harper's magazines, and for John Muir's *Picturesque California* (see Chapter II under year 1888). The year following, having moved to New York City, he became an illustrator for *Cosmopolitan* and *Leslie's* (see Chapter II under year 1889). He was signally honored when engaged by Heber R. Bishop to make nearly one thousand pen-and-ink drawings to illustrate the sumptuous two-volume folio catalogue of carved jade figures (see Fig. 8), the most remarkable collection then known, bequeathed by the merchant-financier in 1902 to the Metropolitan Museum of Art. This task was carried out with a show of virtuosity that has aptly been compared with the etchings of the jades, jewels, and rare glass objects in the Louvre, made by Jules Jacquemart for the French Government.[15] In 1893, according to the Cameron *Observer* of July 13, Burr was continuing to work for Bishop on a new project — illustrations for a catalogue (like the first, for private circulation) of his collection of Oriental porcelains, lacquers, wrought-iron figures, weapons, armor, costumes, etc. (see Fig. 9; also Chapter II under year 1893).

Technical facility, to be sure, had been in high favor with Méryon, Haden, and others; but it played such a subtle role in Burr's subsequent works that one could easily dissociate them, as did Allhusen, from "many of the most beautiful etchings of today, [which] have little beside their technical perfection to recommend them."[16] Will Simmons, a meticulous etcher of wildlife, confessed that "craftsmanship hinders most of us [etchers], who go no farther, lost in our own manual effort; but not so Burr. He simply proves to us that a thing can be well done,

---

[14] E. L. Allhusen, *George Elbert Burr, Etcher* [Denver, c. 1928], p. [5].

[15] Published in Henry Barbet de Jouet, ed., *Musée impérial du Louvre. Les Gemmes et joyaux de la couronne* (Paris, 1865). The *New York Tribune*, in an article "A Superb Book," said that Burr's drawings "showed what really accomplished draftsmanship could make of surfaces whose character photography or even the skill of the artist in color only half interprets. In simple black and white Mr. Burr outlines his forms to perfection, and with the same art gives a conclusive account of textures seen under the play of light and shade. His drawings constitute a rare achievement." (Quoted from the undated pamphlet "Press Comment" cited in n. 9.) Dr. George F. Kunz, vice-president and gem expert of Tiffany & Co., who directed the preparation of the catalogue, stated that "the two great volumes . . . and accompanying descriptive matter fully match the collection itself in magnificence" ("Jade and other Hard Stone Carvings," *Encyclopaedia Britannica*, 14th ed., XII, 865). In this article Kunz did not, however, mention Burr's name.

[16] Op. cit., p. [4].

FIGURE 3 – Burr's early home in Munroe Falls, Ohio.

FIGURE 4 – The Linus E. Burr home in Cameron, Missouri.

Photograph by Burr shortly before he and his wife moved to New York City. In lower left corner, his father and brother Linn; standing against pillar, his sister Bessie.

FIGURE 5 – Elizabeth Rogers Burr.

Photograph by Burr at the Bassett farm c. 1886.
Stake-and-rider fences appear in some of his etchings.

it loses nothing by being beautifully made — could but lose if in the least bit marred in handling. . . . The beauty of craftsmanship is its own reward. . . ."[17]

The key to Burr's successful handling of his subject matter was propounded in 1921 by Lena McCauley, art editor of the *Chicago Evening Post;* she evoked the very faculties that figured in the distinction drawn by Reynolds, pointing out, in praise of Burr's newly completed etchings in the Desert Set, that "beyond the presentment of realities came the flights of the imagination to a poetic interpretation." The analogy to poetry — which at its best offers much more than the skilful contriving of rhyme and meter — may be said to continue as she adds: "No etcher can build his fame on the 'eloquent line' alone unless he has something to say. There must be something more than the picture. . . . Because this is not wisely understood is the reason American etchers as well as American painters have not advanced to higher planes. . . . American portfolios are rich in etchings of architecture and compositions with figures. Few have gone to nature."[18] It was precisely Burr's "philosophical observation of nature," as Millier put it, that imparted subtle and sometimes dramatic qualities to his subjects, spared them from being merely conventional and "traditional," and rendered them, in Burr's own words, "quite different from the usual stock architecture and pastoral farm scenes."[19] Fundamentally he showed an unmistakable kinship to another connoisseur of the arts and of landscape, William Wordsworth, who was "scornful of the poet who would timorously follow man-made rules of art. He calls upon him to let 'Thy Art be Nature; the live current quaff, / And let the groveller sip his stagnant pool' ["A Poet," vv. 5-6]. . . . Wordsworth insists that the true artist, whether painter or poet, must always be free to record his own imaginative reactions and conceptions (if need be, to add 'the light that never was on land or sea'), yet at the same time he must render the essential truth of a given scene. More than anything, a painting must, like all works of art, possess an idea, a thematic mood, a judgment relating it to the inner life."[20] It was the uncommon reach of Burr's sensitivity and productive imagination, and his awareness of his role as artist-poet (see his remarks in Chapter VI under entry #293) that enabled him to achieve effects that astonished and delighted his critics. E. L. Allhusen said of the Desert Set, "It is noteworthy that the subjects chosen are of a type that many etchers would

17 "The Etchings of George Elbert Burr," *Prints,* III (Nov. 1932), 2, 6.

18 "Mr. Burr's Etchings of National Import," in *Chicago Evening Post,* Aug. 16, 1921, sect. "News of the Art World."

19 Letter cited, to Macbeth Gallery.

20 Russell Noyes, *Wordsworth and the Art of Landscape* (Bloomington, Ind., 1968), pp. 60, 63.

reject as unworkable";[21] Malcolm C. Salaman, English art historian and sometime editor of the annual *Fine Prints of the Year*, once wrote to Burr, "You do everything that shouldn't be done, and it's quite right"; and Millier admitted, in another personal letter, "No one ever etched the intangible, or used your techniques before."[22]

Millier's twofold compliment is worthy of remark for another reason. As Burr proceeded from choice of subject matter to finished plate or painting, he drew unerringly upon a gamut of skills that, while they blend in splendid harmony, are individually arresting to the practiced eye; indeed, as we see in Millier's comment, admiring fellow-artists and critics have been less inclined to discriminate between these skills in a way that might suggest that one of them clearly eclipsed the others, than they are to pass quickly from one to another. Thus John Taylor Arms observed that "the [etched] landscapes of George Elbert Burr are marvels of intricate drawing and faultless biting,"[23] and Lena McCauley declared that "no one heretofore has adventured as far in the expression of truth and esthetic values, and used as many methods with success. . . ."[24]

This range of methods, insofar as actual execution is concerned, is best appreciated by those knowledgeable in the techniques of etching. And yet the precise function of each process (e.g., the use of drypoint, in Burr's own words, for "character," aquatint for "subtle poetic effects," soft ground for "shorthand expression of a sudden emotion," etc.), or the tonal beauty and unity of the whole that comes from the combining of, say, aquatint with pure etching or with soft ground, are certainly not lost on the average viewer; neither, to be sure, are the results of Burr's continual experimentation, for example, the variants of #160 *Ragged Pine(s)* and #198 *Prickly Pear Cactus*, or the successive printings of the color etching #44 *Evening, North Wales*.

One can say of Burr's etchings that it is their variety, as well as their exceptional artistic merit, that sets them apart from the commonplace and from sluggish traditionalism; and this is, in turn, a function of the treatment that the artist felt to be appropriate to a given subject. Thus #290 *Nest of the Desert Wren, Arizona* (see Fig. 47), or the studies of cacti or desert mirages, done with the precise delicacy of the miniaturist or artist-naturalist, contrast sharply with #212 *Grand Canyon* [no. 1] (see Fig. 28) in which Burr used, in the words of Edith W. Powell, "a broader, coarser stroke than is his wont . . . striking out for greater size and forcefulness. . . . The flat, geometric pattern of the

---

[21] "George Elbert Burr's Etchings of the Desert," *The Studio*, LXXXIII (Mar. 15, 1922), 144.

[22] Burr cited these excerpts in a letter of Jan. 1, 1930, to R. P. Tolman of the Smithsonian Institution.

[23] *Handbook of Print Making and Print Makers* (New York, 1934), p. 3.

[24] Op. cit.

rocks lends it a distinctly 'modern' appearance."[25] And variety has always sustained the appeal of Burr's etchings to persons of divers tastes who may be attracted by his economy of line and telling use of space reminiscent of Japanese art (#17 *Study of Pines* [no. 3], #178 *Snow Storm, Estes Park,* #214 *From Indio, California*), his exquisite textures (#197 *Whirlwinds, Mojave Desert* [no. 1] [see Fig. 37], #286 *Soapweed, Arizona* [no. 2] [see Fig. 46], #287 *A Mirage, Arizona* [no. 2]), the coldness and desolation of the several winter scenes, his rendering of cloud effects and varied atmospheric phenomena (#82 *High Street, Oxford* [see Fig. 33], #262 *The Desert, Arizona* [no. 2], #139 *Home of the Winds* [no. 2]), the eloquent and imaginative treatment of trees (Mountain Moods series), or landscapes that are now serene (#224 *November*), now unreal and dreamlike (#356 *Old Cedar near Kingman, Arizona* [see Fig. 56]), now grotesque and overpowering (#211 *Needles Mountains, Colorado River, Arizona*).

It goes without saying that Burr's etchings, like his paintings, owed their rich variety primarily to his extensive travels in quest of worthy subjects, which ranged ultimately from delightful Italian cities and antiquities of Sicily to romantic Rhineland castles and rugged North Wales, from the Atlantic seacoast to the Pacific, and from the grandeur of the Colorado mountains to the vast desert regions of the Southwest. If upon occasion Burr found himself drawn to picturesque areas that happened to be time-honored meccas of artist-travelers, the fruits of his labors there were pleasingly free from banality and labored prettiness; indeed, we may attribute much of the enduring appeal that his works have enjoyed to his unerring ability to select subject matter of high artistic merit. A charge of triteness would in fact be tantamount to a denial of beauty in the subject itself, and a repudiation of the general principle laid down more than two centuries ago by Edmund Burke, who held that "when the object of the painting or poem is such as we should run to see if real, let it affect us with what odd sort of sense it will, we may rely upon it, that the power of the poem or picture is more owing to the nature of the thing itself than to the mere effect of imitation or to a consideration of the skill of the imitator, however excellent."[26]

Burr will be esteemed also as an important historian of landscape, for just as Charles Méryon, in his series *Eaux-fortes sur Paris* (1852-1854), recorded the features of ancient streets and buildings that were soon to be sacrificed to Baron Haussmann's urban improvements, so Burr has preserved many an engaging scene that has irrevocably vanished. Examples of this would include sites destroyed in World War II bombings such as those seen in #125 *Catania Gate, Taormina,*

---

[25] "George Elmer [sic] Burr; an Etcher of the Desert," *The Print Connoisseur,* I (June 1921), 312.

[26] *A Philosophical Inquiry into the Origin of Our Ideas of the Sublime and Beautiful* (1756), Part I, sect. xvi, "Imitation."

Sicily (see Fig. 34), #128 *Walpurgiskapelle, Nürnberg,* and #276 *Misty Day, Pauls Wharf, London* (see Fig. 43); changes wrought by time and nature, represented by #51 *Rome from Pincio Garden* and #338 *Mountain of the Holy Cross;* and areas of pristine beauty that have since been transformed by the building of dams and other activities undertaken in the name of progress — #144 *The Rhine at Laufenburg* and various views of rural America, the Front Range of the Rockies, Paradise Valley in Greater Phoenix, and sand-dune regions of southern California.

Burr was a member of the American Institute of Graphic Arts; Arizona Society of Artists; Brooklyn Society of Etchers (renamed Society of American Etchers); Cactus Club, Denver (honorary); California Society of Etchers (charter); Chicago Society of Etchers (charter); Denver Art Association (first president); National Arts Club of New York; New York Society of Etchers; Phoenix Fine Arts Association (president and honorary president); Print Makers' Society of California; Société française aux Etats-Unis.

VALLEY OF THE GUNNISON.

FIGURE 6 — Illustration for Muir's *Picturesque California.*

Pen-and-ink drawing employing picture-within-a-picture device. An artist's brushes stand in jardiniere. From p. 317 of the second volume.

ing process, as in the case of the latter. The Warm Springs valley is of great area, abounding in picturesque drives and romantic rambles, and is surrounded by mountain peaks rising above it 2,000 and 3,000 feet. On Hot Springs Mountain is a virgin forest 150 square miles in extent, abounding in choicest game. These three resorts combined will accommodate about 1,700 guests. Within two miles of Clifton Forge, at Iron Gate, is a new four-story hotel, "Iron Gate Inn," situated on the mountain side overlooking Jackson River, modern in architectural design and in its appointments throughout; the grounds are terraced and gracefully laid out in walks and drives. The principal spring is Lithia, of a fine analysis; it is from this spring that the

of the cottages. From Fort Spring is reached Salt Sulphur Springs, one of the first of the resorts to be founded (1801). Its principal hotel is of stone. The lawn surrounding it is 900 acres in extent. In addition to the sulphur springs there are iodine and bromine springs, efficacious in the treatment of diseases. One of the most wonderful of the springs, in its application to disease, is Red Sulphur, reached from Lowell Station; its waters are most potent in the cure of consumption and bronchial diseases—the only waters of the kind in the world, and many attest their power.

Turning backward to the James River Division reveals the most sublime of nature's wonders, the Natural Bridge of Virginia. This grand arch, builded in mystery, spanning Cedar Creek and

waters are possessed of great virtue when applied to diseases, and which will some day, when capital has touched them with its magic hand, become equally as great to fame.

OLD POINT COMFORT.

OLD Point Comfort, so named by the followers of Captain John Smith in the first part of the seventeenth century because in the quiet waters of Hampton Roads they found a haven of rest and comfort after cruel buffetings of storm and battle, is one of the most delightful spots on the continent, and everywhere are his-

1. IN HOT SPRINGS PARK.   2. BUFFALO GAP, NORTH MOUNTAIN, VA.   3. NATURAL BRIDGE FROM THE WEST.   4. HAWK'S NEST.   5. ON THE NEW RIVER.   6. THE JAMES RIVER AT CLIFTON FORGE.

POINTS OF INTEREST IN THE VIRGINIAS—MAGNIFICENT SCENERY ALONG THE CHESAPEAKE AND OHIO RAILWAY.

table water of the F.F.V. dining-cars is drawn. From Alleghany Station are reached the Old Sweet and Sweet Chalybeate Springs, the former having been a fashionable resort from the time of President Madison. It is a large brick structure with grand ball-room in which the measures of the dance are gracefully tread nightly in season. The queen of resorts is White Sulphur Springs, or "The White," as it is familiarly called by those who frequent it. It is immediately on the line of the Chesapeake and Ohio, and lies in a bowl in the Alleghanies, the mountains rising to a great height on every side. The lawns surrounding the hotel are beautiful, and the drives and walks to "Lovers' Leap" and other romantic nooks are filled with changing scenes. The hotel and surrounding cottages in which the privacy of home life may be secured with the advantages of the springs and hotel, will accommodate 2,500 guests. It is the abode in season of the most eminent from the world of fashion, wealth, and learning. Every State is represented among its guests. The dining-room seats 1,500 guests, and the ball-room is almost as large. For the gay it is the gayest place in the mountains, and yet those who visit it mainly to drink at its fountains and bathe in its pools can have the utmost seclusion and quiet in one

uniting two mountains, is 215 feet in height, 90 feet in width, and 100 feet in length. A county road crosses the bridge, and one in passing over it is not aware of its presence, unless guided by the pathway, he goes to "Pulpit Rock," where he finds himself on its brink. The bridge is one solid rock, with the opening carved out as symmetrically as though done after ages of work by the most skillful of artisans. The views around are entrancing to the eye, and in the vicinity are excellently well-kept hotels, of which there are three, although all under the same management.

The resorts just described are the most prominent only of the famous Springs belt. There are countless others where the

toric associations; and these mingle with and tinge our memories of scenes traversed, until the past and present seem but one. Seated in the world-famed lounging-room, half office and half parlor, of Hygeia Hotel, our eyes drinking in the beauties of this vast sweep of water, listening to the music of the waves and breathing in long, delicious breaths of salt sea-air, Hampton Roads rolls up the beach at our feet; or, lying on the walls of Fortress Monroe, we study the features of this historic coast. Directly opposite is the rocky island and huge stone enclosure of the Rip-raps, or, in vulgar phrase, "Ripp Rapps," built during the Civil War for the custody of Union prisoners. To the left, the

FIGURE 7 — Illustrations for *Frank Leslie's Illustrated Newspaper.*

Wash drawings. Scenes in the Virginias along Chesapeake & Ohio Railway. From issue of July 5, 1890, p. 479.

II

Chronology

NOTE: *No effort has been made to list more than a few representative examples of the countless exhibitions of Burr's paintings and etchings, or of the awards, medals, and honors he received during his lifetime.*

1635 — By this year the first generation of Burr's ancestors to settle in America — Benjamin Burr and William Kelsey in the male line, William Gaylord and John North in the female line — have migrated (some perhaps with families) from south-central England to Connecticut. (The Gaylord line — originally Gaillard — had emigrated to England much earlier from Normandy, where they had been carpenters and shipbuilders.) One may suppose that they had known one another in England, and that they came from similar backgrounds. In their new home they join relatives and friends, and, with newcomers, remain in Connecticut as a homogeneous group for more than a century and a half. Intermarriage is common and marriage between first cousins is not unusual.

Known female surnames absorbed in the direct line are, in their order of occurrence: BURR — Bazey, Hubbard, Porter (originally Porteur), Bailey, Kelsey; KELSEY — Hopkins, Stevens, Graves, Platts, Stevens, Parmelee; GAYLORD — Stebbins, Thompson, Southmayd, Clark, Goodwin, Thomas, North; NORTH — Byrd, Newell, Rice or Royce, Woodford, Wilcox, Savage, Newell. Burr (?–1681) died in Hartford; Kelsey (1600–c. 1680) in Killingworth; Gaylord (1585–1673) in Windsor; North (1615–1691) in a place unknown.

1798 — Linus Burr, the artist's paternal grandfather (6th generation from Benjamin) is born in Haddam, Conn.

1803 — Betsey Kelsey, Burr's paternal grandmother (7th generation from William) is born in North Killingworth, Conn.

1808 — Sylvester Gaylord, Burr's maternal grandfather (8th generation from William) is born in Middletown, Conn.

1817 — Julia North, Burr's maternal grandmother (8th generation from John) is born in Middletown, Conn.; granddaughter of Simeon North of Berlin (Conn.) and Middletown, first civilian maker of flintlock pistols for U.S. Government (see Fig. 1a).

c. 1800 — Joshua Stow, of Middletown, Conn., commissary in General Moses Cleaveland's party surveying the Western Reserve in 1796, purchases from the state of Connecticut, with other persons, Town 3, Range 10 — a twenty-five-mile square located ninety-five miles west of the Pennsylvania line. This, henceforth known as Stow Township, will include Stow Corners (now Stow), Florence (later renamed Munroe Falls), and part of the present town of Cuyahoga Falls. Hudson, settled in 1802, lies to the north (in Town 4, Range 10) and Tallmadge to the south (Town 2, Range 10). Joshua Stow begins to sell portions of this property to relatives and friends living in or near Middletown.

1803 — Ohio is admitted to the Union.

1809 — Sylvester Gaylord, Burr's maternal grandfather, joins the great migration to the Western Reserve when he is brought by oxcart, at the age of nine months, to Florence, O., a journey of forty-one days. This locality offers many advantages to the early settlers: plentiful water (the Cuyahoga River with its falls for generating power, many springs and spring-fed lakes and streams, and deep wells), outcroppings of coal in the Tallmadge hills, and, within a day's trip by wagon, salt beds.

1830s — In this decade the brothers Munroe (spelled by some historians "Monroe"), of near-by Boston Township (just west of Hudson Township), form a syndicate, buy all available businesses around Florence (including a chair factory and the flourishing mills on the Cuyahoga River) and most of the town itself, which they rename Munroe Falls. They propose to build a self-sustaining and strictly regulated Utopian community and trading center for the surrounding country; they have mulberry trees and silkworms brought in by Conestoga wagons, hoping to establish a mill like those back East. The grandiose scheme attracts the curious from as far away as Boston, but soon goes the way of all Utopias; in its general collapse, hastened by the panic of 1837, the bank and businesses fail and the disillusioned move away, leaving behind the more independent first settlers and their families.

14

FIGURE 8 — Pen-and-ink drawing of jade bowl, Heber R. Bishop catalogue. From p. 123 of the second volume (Fig. 368).

FIGURE 9 — Pen-and-ink drawing of wrought-iron figure, Bishop collection.

Articulated flying monster. From New York National Academy of Design exhibition catalogue, 1893.

1834 — Linus Edwin Burr, the artist's father, is born in Middletown, Conn.

1840 — Lucy Ellen Gaylord, the artist's mother, is born in Munroe Falls.

1855 — Linus Edwin Burr moves from Connecticut to Munroe Falls, where the Norths (relatives of his future wife) own a hoe manufactory, and begins to buy property there.

1857 — In December a marriage license is issued to Linus Edwin Burr and Lucy Ellen Gaylord, then aged seventeen, the eldest of five siblings born of Sylvester Gaylord's second marriage.

1859 — George Elbert Burr is born on April 14 at Munroe Falls, probably in the house of his mother's parents, the Sylvester Gaylords.

1860 — Elizabeth Rogers, Burr's future wife, is born in Kentucky on February 14.

1861 — Two days before Burr's second birthday, Fort Sumter is fired upon, and two months later his baby sister dies. His father, with wife and son, goes to live with his widowed mother in Middletown. William Gaylord, brother of George Elbert's mother, joins Union Army; three years later her half-brother, Sylvester Gaylord (Jr.), joins Union Navy.

1865 — They return to their former home in Munroe Falls (see Fig. 3). Built c. 1813 by William Stow, son of the first proprietor of Stow Township, it stands on the south side of the Munroe Falls-Cuyahoga Falls road just west of its juncture with the north-south road from Hudson to Tallmadge. The property, lying on both sides of the road, is crossed by the Cuyahoga River and the Pennsylvania and Ohio Canal. George Elbert has already begun to draw and paint; an attic room in his Gaylord grandparents' home close by serves as a studio for him and his mother. He attends the Union District School in Munroe Falls.

1868 — Death of the French etcher Charles Méryon (b. 1837).

1869 — Burr's father sells the Munroe Falls property, joins the great migration that attends the opening of the West, and moves his family to Cameron, Mo., a community divided in its sympathies during the Civil War, for many years an important collection center for livestock marketing, and crossroad for people coming from the East or up the Mississippi and Missouri en route to the western gold fields. It is on the Hannibal & St. Joseph railroad (pony express went west from St. Joseph 1860–61) and the Kansas City Branch, and, after 1871, the Chicago, Rock Island & Pacific. (Missouri has been a state since 1821.)

There Linus Burr opens a store (L. E. Burr, Hardware), one of the earliest and most successful businesses in Cameron, and builds a comfortable house on the edge of town, at the end of a tree-lined drive and on a rise of ground three hundred feet back from the highway near the intersection of the Packard Cemetery road (see Fig. 4). The Burrs attend the Christian Church.

1871 — A disastrous fire destroys forty-five buildings including the hardware store. Linus continues the business in a new location; it adds a tinshop in which George Elbert, who now attends public school in Cameron, is soon to print #364 [My First Etching] and #365 [My Second Attempt at Etching].

1876 — "Bertie Burr has just built a new greenhouse at his father's residence . . . , filled with a fine lot of house and bedding plants, hanging baskets, etc. He now has on hand between 200 and 300 varieties, including nearly every kind known in this climate, [and] has built up a good trade in this line . . ." (Cameron *Observer*, May 26). Bessie Burr, the artist's sister, is born in Cameron. George Elbert is now seventeen years old.

1877 — At the end of February, Elder (i.e., Reverend) William C. Rogers of the Christian Church, his wife, three sons, and two daughters, move to Cameron from St. Joseph, Mo. Elizabeth, the older daughter, will become Burr's wife. In October, George Elbert leaves for Oskaloosa, Ia., to attend business college. (The Cameron high school has not at this date graduated its first class.)

1878 — On December 30 Burr leaves for study at the Chicago Academy of Design (later renamed the Art Institute of Chicago). His mother's sister Charlotte (then Mrs. Henshaw) is studying there also.

1879 — On January 2 Elizabeth Rogers leaves to attend Oskaloosa College (Christian) in Oskaloosa, Ia. Around April 1 Burr terminates his brief art studies in Chicago and returns to Cameron.

1880 — Burr makes a wash drawing of Elizabeth Rogers standing against a tree. After celebrating their golden-wedding anniversary he inscribes it "My Pal, 1880-1935." In a letter of July 30, 1940, Mrs. Burr will hark back to "sixty years of a close companionship" and allude to the year 1880, after which she and her late husband were "four years chums with hardly a thought of getting married."

1881 — Burr & Corn Hardware (Silas H. Corn, a local lawyer, becomes a silent partner until his retirement in 1886) move into their own building at the southeast corner of Third and Chestnut streets; it measures 90 x 40 feet, has three stories and a full basement. They sell builders' supplies, roofing, tinware, carloads of heating stoves, cook-stoves, and barbed wire, kitchenware, threshing machines and other heavy farm machinery, buggies, and spring wagons. George Elbert works in his father's store, but spends much time roaming over the countryside, sketching and traveling about on his father's railroad pass. Linn W. Burr, the artist's brother, is born in Cameron, twenty-two years his junior. Linn and Bessie are the only two of George Elbert's six siblings to survive.

1883 — "Burt Burr left yesterday morning for his annual trip to Chicago and over the lakes" (Cameron *Observer*, Aug. 9). During this month-long respite from hay fever (see below under years 1886, 1896), he apparently visits his Aunt Charlotte (now Mrs. J. H. Banning) in South Bend, Ind., where, according to the South Bend *Tribune* (quoted in the *Observer*), he makes several sketches along the St. Joseph River near St. Mary's Academy and "along the wooded lane leading from Notre Dame to St. Mary's."

1884 — On May 1, in the Cameron Christian Church, George Elbert is married to Elizabeth Rogers (see Fig. 5) by the bride's father, and a reception follows in L. E. Burr's "elegant and commodious home." In September he is in Chicago buying goods for the hardware store.

1885 — He is conducting a class in drawing. He sends some of his own drawings to Harper Bros. and receives a letter from Charles Parsons, superintendent of their art department, "speaking in high terms of his work" (Cameron *Observer*, Feb. 12).

1886 — Mrs. Burr is engaged to teach summer school in the Shreve district south of Cameron. "George Elbert is having a hundred or more of his best sketches framed preparatory to placing them on exhibition and sale" in Hemingway's Photograph Gallery (Cameron *Observer*, May 13). In July the Burrs go "to the lake regions for the improvement of Mr. Burr's health," where they remain until early September. In November he and his father lease from B. F. Bassett several hundred acres of meadowland on the south edge of Cameron.

1887 — Burr travels during the month of December to New York, Boston, and other eastern points, primarily (it may be assumed) to find employment in the art world.

1888 — Still in Cameron, he is doing art work for both Harper's and Scribner's magazines, and his first signed illustrations (see Fig. 6) appear in Volume II of John Muir's *Picturesque California* (Chapters XVII, "Washington and Puget Sound," and XVIII, "Colorado"). It is

FIGURE 10 — The artist and his wife in Switzerland.

19

not until December 27 that the *Observer* announces that Burr "will soon depart for New York City to spend several months and will be joined by his wife in a few weeks. . . ." They take a small apartment near the Museum of Natural History; Burr mingles with artists, attends exhibitions and lectures, goes on sketching trips outside the city.

1889 — For ten months, signed drawings appear in *The Cosmopolitan* as illustrations for articles, poems, and occasional tailpieces (see issues of April, May, June, September, November, December; also January 1890). Signed illustrations appear in *Frank Leslie's Illustrated Newspaper* and continue through 1892; they consist of pen-and-ink and wash drawings, made from staff photographs and sketches sent in from various places. Subjects include newsworthy events, new buildings and industries, mining sites, etc. Burr's interest in etching continues; he attends "the last exhibit of the last surviving Etching society of that day," the New York Etching Club, founded in 1877 (letter of Feb. 29, 1932, to Mrs. Bertha E. Jaques, an etcher and secretary of the Chicago Society of Etchers).

FIGURE 11 — Burr's apartment and first studio, Toms River, New Jersey. Probably photographed by the artist.

1890 — Burr travels for *Leslie's* to Virginia, Chicago, Dallas, etc.; sends back photographs and sketches to be prepared for printing by other staff artists, also his own pen-and-ink and wash drawings made on the spot (see Fig. 7).

1891 — As special staff artist for *Leslie's*, accompanies President Benjamin Harrison and party on ten-thousand-mile tour through the South, Southwest, and to the Pacific coast, sending back for publication sketches, finished drawings, and photographs.

1893 — In a special article, "G. E. Burr's Work," following a personal interview in Cameron, the *Observer* of July 13 reports: "He has recently finished drawings of jade carvings collected by a wealthy New York gentleman, for which he received over $3,000." These were the thousand or so pen-and-ink drawings made for Heber R. Bishop in his Fifth Ave. residence over a period of several years. The elephant folio catalogue in which they were to appear (already mentioned in Chapter I) cost Bishop, says the article, $75,000 for one hundred

FIGURE 12. *#95 Barnegat Light* 5 x 8 inches

Figure on boat suggests a sly self-portrait. *Courtesy of the Denver Public Library*

FIGURE 13 — Brinton Terrace, the Burrs' first home in Denver.

copies. "They will be donated to the leading libraries of the world, but none will be for sale." The article continues: "Mr. Burr is now doing another big job . . . , illustrations for [Bishop's] private collection of porcelains, bronzes and lacquers, for which he will receive about $5,000. These drawings are also for publication in book form for private circulation." I have been unable to find evidence that this second work was ever published, but many of the intended illustrations were used in the executors' sale catalogue edited in 1906 by Thomas E. Kirby. (A copy of this limited edition can be seen in the Denver Public Library.) Another public sale that included some of Bishop's Oriental porcelains, bronzes, etc., was held in New York in 1911 by the Anderson Auction Co., whose catalogue contains none of Burr's drawings.

1896 — In the spring, Burr, with his wife, leaves for Europe on the North German Lloyd S.S. *Kaiser Wilhelm II*, and for four and a half years travels from Sicily to North Wales, sketching and painting (see Fig. 10). Just before he sails, the Grolier Club in New York exhibits his drawings made for the Heber Bishop catalogue. Reaching Venice, they take a room for five weeks with an Italian family near the Piazza of St. Mark, with a view, from their balcony, of the Bridge of Sighs. They spend October in the island city of Chioggia (some eighteen miles south at lower end of the lagoon), where they find picturesque fishing boats carrying red and yellow sails that remind the artist, at a distance, of a flock of butterflies. In letters home he remarks, apropos of his sketching and painting, that he is getting a new hold on color. "There is no blue that is so changeable, so full of palpitating light as that above us here, while the water . . . mimics the sky and assumes

FIGURE 14 — The Burrs' mountain cabin near Denver.

FIGURE 15 — Studio-home on Logan Street, Denver.

FIGURE 16 — Burr in his Logan Street studio.

Used by the Burrs as Christmas card, 1914. *From the collection of the Honolulu Academy of Arts*

still stranger combinations of color." He reports to his father on November 1 that he has not had hay fever this year — his first escape from "that miserable scourge" in fifteen years.

1899 — The Burrs spend the winter of 1899–1900 in Oxford, then return to Venice via Switzerland and lease a modest three-room apartment.

1900 — In Venice, receives $195 from his mother, enabling him and his wife to "rest easy for a time." (Mrs. Burr cooks on a portable alcohol burner, pays four or five cents for a week's supply of flowers, and twenty-eight cents each for chickens.) After several weeks they go to England via Austria and the Paris Exposition, and sail for New York November 3 from Liverpool on the Cunard S.S. *Lucania.*

1901 — The Burrs are occupying a small apartment in a private home in Toms River, N.J., with a studio in a flower garden tended by the artist (see Fig. 11). A friend remarks, "I believe you could make a clothes pole grow if you put it in the ground" (letter of Dec. 31, 1940, from Mrs. Burr to Linn Burr's wife Eva). Burr is earning his living by selling watercolors and etchings.

1903 — Death of James McNeill Whistler (b. 1834).

1904 — Burr is currently listed in *American Art Annual* as "painter, illustrator." Makes his "first successful color etching," #39 *Florence from Monte Oliveto* [no. 1].

1905 — Thirty-nine of Burr's watercolors are shown in a special exhibition (Feb. 20–Mar. 18) in Klackner Gallery, New York City.

1906 — Forty-eight Burr watercolors are exhibited (Apr. 2–14) by Dunton & Gardner, of Boston. At about the same time, others are shown in Kansas City, Mo., seventy at Fenton & Stair's Gallery in Cleveland, and some sixty at Earle's Galleries in Philadelphia. (Some catalogues of early exhibitions are undated, others are not available.) The Burrs travel that fall to Denver hoping to find a more healthful climate, and within a few months decide to move there permanently. They live first in downtown Brinton Terrace, Denver's "Greenwich Village" — an attractive English-style multiple-unit building, since demolished (see Fig. 13). Here also the Boutwell brothers open an art gallery; their first exhibit consists of Burr's watercolors of European subjects — his first one-man show in Denver. The Burrs attend the Unitarian Church, of which Dr. David Utter, a cousin of Mrs. Burr, is pastor.

1907 — His second one-man show at the same gallery — watercolors of California and Colorado, and five color etchings.

Figure 17 — Burr at his hand press.

Photograph dated 1919. On this press, which required great strength, Burr printed Mountain Moods and the Desert Set.

1909 — Burr designs and builds a studio-home at 1325 Logan St. (see Fig. 15); it has small living quarters and a spacious story-and-a-half studio with a good north light, fireplace, mission furniture, Oriental rugs, shawls draped over railings, peacock feathers — all in the style of the day (see Fig. 16).

1910 — His color etchings continue to appear with his watercolors in one-man shows and exhibitions. He is the first president of the Denver Art Association, and active in art circles and on committees and art juries. The Burrs have been frequent guests at the Boutwell's mountain cabin, and soon build their own in the foothills of the Front Range on property owned by the Pick-Up Club (see Fig. 14). ("Pick-Up Cabin" — or simply "The Shack" — stood above Eldorado Springs just south of Boulder and some twenty-five miles south of Longs Peak; it was near Tunnel 7 of the Moffat Road branch of the Denver and Rio Grande Western Railroad, not finished until after the Burrs had left Colorado.) As long as weather permits, they spend their summers in this unspoiled area that affords grand vistas of forests, plains, and vast skies. Death of Sir Francis Seymour Haden (b. 1818).

1911 — Death of the French etcher Alphonse Legros (b. 1837).

1913 — New York Society of Etchers founded. Burr becomes a member.

1914 — Forty-nine black-and-white and twenty-two color etchings on sale at Carl J. Smalley gallery, McPherson, Kansas.

1915 — Color etchings are among twenty-two shown at Panama-Pacific International Exposition in San Francisco. Brooklyn Society of Etchers founded; later renamed Society of American Etchers. Burr will become a member.

1916 — Exhibits two etchings in First Annual Exhibition of Brooklyn Society of Etchers, at Brooklyn Museum, Nov. 28–Dec. 31: #62 *Winter* [no. 1], a drypoint, and #104 *The Rhine below St. Goar,* a soft ground. #137 *Winter Morning* is awarded a silver medal by the St. Paul (Minnesota) Institute. Exhibits his Mountain Moods series (see Chapter III) in his studio-home.

1918 — "George Elbert Burr, who was busy making etchings through the summer and autumn, sending them to exhibitions in Brooklyn, New York, Philadelphia, Pittsburgh, Detroit, and Chicago, is now painting in watercolors, in the technique of which medium he excels" (*The Denver News,* May 12).

FIGURE 18 — The Burr's first home in Phoenix.

FIGURE 19 — The Burrs' second home in Phoenix.

The studio is visible behind the house.

1919 — "In fifteen of the larger cities [Burr] has had 'one-man' shows, and in some of these he shows his work annually" (*The Denver News*, Mar. 2, quoting from T. M. Fisher's current article in *The American Magazine of Art*). He is invited by Stephen J. Mather, director of the National Park Service, to go with the Sierra Club, in July of the following year, into the unexplored part of Yosemite National Park and to do a series of etchings of this region. The invitation is regretfully declined. At Colorado State Fair #137 *Winter Morning* wins first prize for etchings; #76 *Street in San Remo* (see Fig. 32) wins second prize. On December 28 Reginald Poland, in his column in *Rocky Mountain News*, expresses an *idée fixe* of some art critics when he reports that Burr "has returned to more important oil paintings, [and] has sold in Chicago, within the month, four out of five canvases exhibited there." He adds: "He has been quite unable to supply the many demands for his etchings."

1920 — The Burrs visit Tucson.

1921 — Burr copyrights the last of the thirty-five etchings in the Desert Set (see Chapter III), which is sent out as a traveling exhibition by the American Federation of Arts.

1922 — An exhibition of his watercolors in Denver attracts much attention, and fifteen paintings are sold within a week (*Rocky Mountain News*, June 4). In poor health, Burr spends the winter in Tucson.

1923 — Spends the winter in a tiny apartment in Phoenix. Watercolors of the desert shown in Denver Public Library.

1924 — Writes on April 12 from the Fontenelle Apartments, Phoenix, to a Dr. and Mrs. Rutherford, mentioning his poor health; he hopes "in a few weeks to be able to sketch some." Although unable to do vigorous work, he finds recreation in making a number of pastels in the Painted Desert before returning to Denver (see Fig. 29). Sells his home and moves to Phoenix, residing first at 72 West Moreland St. Uses photograph of this house, with Mrs. Burr sitting on porch step, as Christmas card (see Fig. 18, a similar view). In art exhibit at Arizona State Fair wins first prize in watercolor and first prize in etching (see, in Chapter VI, #212 *Grand Canyon* [no. 1], also Fig. 28). Etchings shown at Smithsonian Institution, Oct. 29–Nov. 28.

1925 — On April 4 at organization meeting of the Phoenix Fine Arts Association (the antecedent of the present Phoenix Art Museum) Burr is appointed to the committee on constitution and bylaws, and elected to the Board of Governors. His etchings again exhibited at the Smithsonian. Writes on August 9 to R. P. Tolman, Assistant Curator, Division of Graphic Arts, "I am gaining in strength, but it is slow. Hope

FIGURE 20 — Studio portrait of the artist.

Photographer unknown. *Courtesy of Taylor Studios & Camera Shop, Cameron, Mo.*

FIGURE 21 — The artist at his brother Linn's home in Cameron, Missouri.

this winter to have a new home and a studio here, and be able to do some work once more." Buys small house at 70 West Lynwood St. (see Fig. 19); has fifty roses in his garden. First exhibition in Phoenix held Dec. 7–24 at the Miller-Sterling Gallery; it contains ninety-eight etchings, some of which have been shown recently at the Corcoran Gallery of Art in Washington. A reception is to follow. "I am not fit for it," he writes to his brother on December 7; "wish I was in bed in Cameron, in the moon, or some place where I could forget work for one week and get rested. . . . However, will try to look pleasant, and be a good boy."

1927 — Exhibition and sale of forty etchings of the Great American Desert at Doll & Richards, Boston, Feb. 14–Mar. 5. On May 23 writes to Frank Weitenkampf, Curator of Prints at the New York Public Library, "Not as husky as of the days before the flu, and soon tire," and to his brother, on December 20, "Have been completely down and out for a few days. Too much work, and some annoyances."

1928 — Burr is president of the Phoenix Fine Arts Association. The city has its first major art exhibition, to which the American Federation of Arts adds some twenty works by Frederick Waugh, Robert Henri, Herbert Dunton, Ernest Lawson, Edward Redfield, and others. Four thousand people attend, according to John P. Frank in his history of the Phoenix Art Museum. In July Burr's etchings are selected for an exhibition of contemporary artists held in the Bibliothèque Nationale, Paris, and #262 *The Desert, Arizona* [no. 2] is retained for its permanent collection. Receives a clipping from the London *Times* in a letter from Campbell Dodgson, Keeper of Prints in the British Museum, who has arranged "a large showing of my work now on exhibit" there (letter to Tolman, Dec. 18, 1929).

1929 — An exhibition in the Library of Congress of etchings by Daniel Garber, Frank Duveneck, and others, contains nine of Burr's winter scenes. In London the Victoria & Albert Museum exhibits his etchings. He is elected honorary president of the Phoenix Fine Arts Association "in token of our grateful acknowledgment of his wise leadership during the growth of the organization."

1930 — In Washington the National Museum shows fifty of his desert prints; the Smithsonian Institution exhibits his drypoints and aquatints. He has sold about two thousand dollars worth of prints within four months (letter to Tolman, Jan. 30). Informs Mrs. Jaques (letter of Nov. 10) that he has put over 700 prints into mats and sent them to dealers, and adds, "Was quite ill for seven weeks in Pasadena this summer."

1931 — In October, the Desert Set is shown at McKlees Galleries, Philadelphia. #325 *Superstition Mountain, Apache Trail, Arizona, Night* [no. 2] (see Fig. 51) is exhibited at Brooklyn Museum, Nov. 17–Dec. 31, among American etchings to be published in the 1931 edition of *Fine Prints of the Year* (London). Estimates that over 600 of his etchings are now in museum collections (letter of Oct. 6 to Curator of Prints, Brooklyn Museum).

1932 — The Desert Set is exhibited in Goodspeed's Book Shop, Boston. Sends to Mrs. Jaques (letter of Feb. 29) list of awards, exhibitions, and honors accorded his etching #325 *Superstition Mountain, Apache Trail, Arizona, Night* [no. 2] — all within a period of three months: Art Alliance; Society of American Etchers; Philadelphia Society of Etchers; American Etchers, Philadelphia; National Academy; Boston Print Club; California Print Makers; Institute of Graphic Arts (one of two honorable mentions in group of 165 prints by 40 artists); selected for *Fifty Prints of the Year;* reproduced in *Fine Prints of the Year* (London), *One Hundred Best American Prints,* and *100 Prints of the Year* (London).

1934 — Writes on March 5 to Leila Mechlin, secretary of the American Federation of Arts: ". . . I am still having a lot of fun with my work, when I am able to be up and around. Have finished quite a lot of new plates in the past three years, and water colors as well. A number of new prints have attracted considerable attention, which is pleasant. Most of the twenty-five new plates, I've printed in very limited editions, of from four to ten prints, and have destroyed the plates; in that way I have the joy of creation, without the real work of printing. None of these have yet been given to the dealers — next year, perhaps, I will show them. . . ." Receives an honorable mention from Philadelphia Print Club.

1935 — Comments in a letter of November 29 to Weitenkampf on the many plates he has etched. "It looks like an awful lot, now I am so tired. I can't imagine how I did it, in addition to hundreds of water colors. However, last winter I painted fifteen good-size Water Colors, 15 x 20 to 22 x 28 in. — and they all sold but one. Now I am anxious to paint again. But the flesh is weak."

1936 — Letter of April 3 to Weitenkampf: "Thanks for the proofs of notices just received. I also read in my [New York] *Times* a notice of the show. . . . Have been 'awfully' busy this year, sending out prints to replace those sold, as my dealers have sold over four thousand dollars worth of my Etchings since January first." Letter of May 25 to the same: "Had a splendid winter, so far as 'business' goes, but, although it's flattering to have dealers sell a lot of my work, still I am

FIGURE 22 — The Burr plot in Old Packard Cemetery, Cameron, Missouri.

a bit weary of business — have some work still in the stage of 'growing pains,' and hope to get some pleasure soon in finishing it."

1939 — Burr dies peacefully on November 17 at the age of eighty. Reminiscing a year later in letters to Eva Burr, Mrs. Burr recalls one of her husband's last requests: "Open the curtains all the way so I can see the sky; then open both French doors to the sleeping porch so that I can see the studio and the trees back of it." She adds that he had instructed her to destroy certain packages of papers. Burr's ashes are buried in the old Packard Cemetery in Cameron, Mo., following an Episcopal service in Phoenix.

1943 — Mrs. Burr dies; her ashes are buried next to her husband's. A marker of red Missouri granite stands over their graves, in a simple setting beneath an overhanging red cedar tree (see Fig. 22).

George Elbert Burr   Del. et Imp.   No. 54

FIGURE 23 — #40 *Rheinstein Castle*   9⅜ x 6⅛ inches   Color etching

III

Three Notable Groups
of Etchings

1. COLOR ETCHINGS

AT THE TURN OF THE CENTURY, Burr, accompanied by his wife, spent nearly five years abroad, sketching and painting in various parts of Switzerland (see Fig. 10), Italy, Sicily, Germany, England, and North Wales — a long sojourn that offered infinite opportunities to study landscapes and ancient landmarks, clouds, color, and light. On his return to the States he considered himself primarily an accomplished watercolorist; he was, in fact, listed in early art directories as "painter," and as late as 1908, two years after taking up residence in Denver, it was said that "his time has been given almost altogether to water color, in which branch he has achieved his greatest fame."[1] But even then he had been turning more and more to etching, and his portfolio bulged with sketches of European scenes that were to supply this medium so liberally that in the end they represented no less than thirty percent of his total copper plates. His visit to Nürnberg (Dürer's birthplace) may well have played a part in rekindling his interest in etching, and a leisurely journey to Heidelberg and through the romantic Rhine country, as well as his curiosity about early German experiments in color etching, most certainly aroused a desire to try his hand at that exacting and challenging medium. At the same time, his demonstrated skill as a watercolorist had abundantly satisfied the generally held principle that "it is essential that the color etcher should have experience in painting."[2]

---

[1] Sheldon Cheney, "Notable Western Etchers," *Sunset,* XXI (Dec. 1908), 740.
[2] George E. Senseney, "Etching in Color," *Palette & Bench,* II (May 1910), 192.

At the end of these productive years abroad, Burr settled in the small resort town of Toms River, New Jersey, which offered him many advantages as a nature-lover as well as easy access to New York City. He soon established himself in the mainstream of art, exhibiting watercolors in New York, Denver, Boston and elsewhere, and earning his livelihood from the sale of both these and black-and-white etchings. It was in Toms River, in 1904, that he made what he called his "first successful color etching," #39 *Florence from Monte Oliveto* [no. 1]. (Color impressions from this plate can be seen in the Phoenix Art Museum, the Denver Public Library, and the Library of Congress.) His "first experiment in color" after moving to Denver in 1906, at the age of forty-seven, was #42 *Piñon Trees and Spanish Peaks, Colorado* (see Fig. 24). (Copies of this are in the aforementioned locations and in the New York Public Library.) An announcement that he was then etching "principally . . . in colors"[3] must be understood as an allusion to his continual experimentation in this self-taught technique, not to the number of color etchings produced, which, actually, was quite small. Morris R. Ward, too, remarked several years later that after going to Denver "color etching occupied most of [Burr's] time"; but, he added, "it was only after several years of hard labour that he succeeded in mastering the intricate difficulties of the art."[4] Thus in 1907 only five color etchings were exhibited, along with his watercolors, in Boutwell's Arts & Crafts Studio in Brinton Terrace;[5] and in 1908 Cheney stated that "the number of his [color] plates is very limited, the prints of only five . . . have been placed before the public."[6]

In this exceptional field Burr was not only a virtuoso, but a pioneer as well. Cheney regarded color etching as "practically a new art,"[7] and an editorial in *Palette & Bench* spoke of it two years later as "an art which has attained considerable popularity in Germany and France, but has so far been attempted by but few American artists."[8] It was fifteen years after Burr had made his first color etching that Theodore Merrill Fisher could observe that, owing to "the inherent difficulties of production demanding . . . not only unusual artistic ability but infinite pains and most exact and intimate knowledge of the process, the devotees of the color plate are in their entirety only a small group."[9]

Fisher correctly viewed color etching as "a means of expression which each aspirant apparently must make his own by self-training and individual mastery. This is true not only because there are so few from whom he may learn the art-science, but because if the final

---

3 *The Denver Post*, Oct. 21, 1906.

4 "The Etchings of George Elbert Burr," *The International Studio*, LIV (Nov. 1914), 11.

5 *The Denver Post*, Dec. 4, 1907.

6 Loc. cit.

7 Loc. cit.

8 II (May 1910), 187.

9 "George Elbert Burr," *The American Magazine of Art*, X (Feb. 1919), 127–28.

results are to be what they should be, namely, individual tokens of his genius, he must of necessity handle even the mechanics of the process in a personal way. Burr has done exactly this."[10] And his process aroused so much interest that, according to the *Denver Post* of October 21, 1906, it had been "inquired about by nearly every water-color artist in America." Fortunately, its description is preserved in the Denver Public Library, prepared by Burr himself "in reply to many inquiries" and printed on a small sheet, probably for distribution at the early Denver exhibitions:

> . . . I first etch the plate in line as for an ordinary black-and-white etching, and after taking a proof, I [apply] ground [to] the plate with resin powder and then etch in aquatint for the different colors and tones; or I first start the plate with soft-ground etching and afterward finish with aquatint.
>
> After the plate is properly etched, I then paint the picture on the copper with ordinary oil colors, removing carefully all color that does not adhere to the granulated surface, and then print on moistened sheet of Japan paper in ordinary etching press.
>
> By this method each print is a distinct picture, each proof requiring a separate painting on the copper, no two being alike, the pictures varying according to the mood and will of the artist.
>
> The process is a slow one and I make a very limited number of proofs and then destroy the plate, by that means giving added value to the few prints that I place before the public.

Burr much preferred his own independently developed process to the one described by his contemporary George Senseney, which consisted of printing only one color at a time, then superimposing or adding colors — a method that involved much blocking out and perhaps four printings to obtain one finished etching.[11] Senseney believed that "almost any kind of an etched plate is capable of interpretation in color printing"; that "in the plate for color etching several processes can be combined to advantage"; and that the most satisfied artist is he who does his own printing.[12] These ideas Burr heartily concurred with and always practiced, though he disagreed with Senseney's process. It obviously delighted him to discover, as it were, this transitional bridge between the delicate medium of watercolor and etching in black and white, and to master his own exacting technique. Also, as he infers in his prepared statement, repeated changes in a given plate

---

10 Ibid., p. 128.

11 Morris R. Ward remarked (op. cit., pp. 11, 12) that "at bottom, [Burr's] methods differ to some extent from those in most general use among his contemporaries in the art," and that they demand "the continual artistic skill and ability of the artist himself." The multiple-plate process was then being used in England, Ward said, by Nelson Dawes and Lee Hankey.

12 "Etching in Color," p. 194.

permitted an agreeable degree of artistic freedom and creative enjoyment; and the painting of the plate had infinitely greater appeal than did the comparative drudgery of reprinting the same one again and again in black and white.[13]

His successes in this medium received frequent notices in the Denver press and elsewhere. Sheldon Cheney's article in *Sunset* reproduced #40 *Rheinstein Castle* (see Fig. 23) in black and white under the title *A Study of the Rheinstein*. In a letter dated October 19, 1913, Morris Ward informed Frank Weitenkampf, then head of the Print Room of the New York Public Library, that Burr was "preparing two complete sets of his color etchings . . . for exhibition under the auspices of the California Society of Etchers and the Chicago Society of Etchers of both of which he is a charter member." The *Denver Post* on November 18, 1914, stated that Burr's color etchings had been sent away for display at the Panama-Pacific International Exposition, which opened in San Francisco in February 1915. The *New York Evening Post* of December 17, 1923, reviewing an exhibition of etchings in the Brooklyn Museum, commented on Burr's flair for color, referring to #214 *From Indio, California*, "one of the novelties of a collection of 287 items." The same year, Hugh Walpole, the English novelist and print connoisseur, purchased at Colorado Springs a copy of #68 *Arizona Clouds* [no. 1], in color — already a rarity, for the plate had been destroyed.[14]

By 1923 Burr had completed not only his Mountain Moods (Estes Park) series, consisting of paired watercolors and black-and-white etchings, but also his taxing Desert Set, and was shortly to move, for reasons of health, to Phoenix. Four color etchings made from plates of the Desert Set, which may be regarded essentially as experimental, seem to mark the end of his activity in that category — a step so patently irrevocable as to attract public notice and comment.[15] It should be noted, incidentally, that Burr had developed such consummate technical skill that, without resorting to oils, he was able, using only one color of ink, to imply and suggest color merely through delicacy

---

[13] Ward (op. cit., p. 12) applauded the "great variety of effort" to be found "in the various proofs of any one plate. This lends a certain atmosphere of novelty and permits a large range of treatment in a plate, by which it may be made to represent the same scene at different hours or seasons." For a good example of this, see the description of #138 *Spanish Peaks* [no. 2] in Chapter VI. Burr remarked (*The Denver Post*, Nov. 18, 1914), "In a water color the tones of nature must be faithfully depicted, but not in etching. Of course you never saw a pea-green sky, but if it's lovely, no one cares."

[14] *Rocky Mountain News*, Apr. 13, 1923. Walpole spent the morning of the 12th in Burr's Denver studio on Logan Street, where "the artist drew off three prints for the author's enjoyment and instruction" and showed him "nearly a hundred prints done in every medium known to the etcher. . . ."

[15] *Rocky Mountain News* (loc. cit.) mentions Burr's "withdrawal . . . from work in color," and five years later E. L. Allhusen, in his *George Elbert Burr, Etcher* [Denver, c. 1928], p. [4], stated that color etching was "a process which Mr. Burr has abandoned."

George Elbert Burr

Figure 24 — #42 *Piñon Trees and Spanish Peaks, Colorado*   6⅛ x 9⅜ inches   Color etching

of line and by various combinations of the etching processes. Prints in this category should not be mistaken for color etchings.

The best and largest collection of Burr's color etchings that I have seen is in the Phoenix Art Museum. These superb impressions, the gift of Mr. and Mrs. Walter R. Bimson, include many choice items not on public view elsewhere. The entire group, long withheld from circulation by the Burrs for their own enjoyment, was purchased from the artist toward the end of his life. The Denver Public Library collection, which is still growing, was started by a gift from Mr. and Mrs. A. Reynolds Morse; it includes some twelve color etchings, plus a few black-and-white prints pulled from plates used also for color. Other sizeable public collections of Burr etchings include few in color — six or eight at the most — or none at all.

Owing to the artist's typical indifference to recording precise data and keeping records, much information pertaining to the color etchings is wanting or unavailable. Many copies are untitled and must be identified by other means. The exact number of prints made in color from a given plate is usually unknown; many copies have long since passed into private hands, and Burr's indefinite notations such as "20 or 25 in color" obscure as well the number of impressions struck in black and white from the same plate. Also, it is impossible to determine how many individual plates may have been tried at one time or another in color. Trial proofs may be found either in color or in black and white.

I have examined the following thirty-three color etchings with one exception: the American Etchers series, Volume VII, places #84 in this category, but I have seen it only in black and white.

38 *Rome from Palatine Hill*
39 *Florence from Monte Oliveto* [no. 1]
40 *Rheinstein Castle* (see Fig. 23)
41 *Marksburg Castle*
42 *Piñon Trees and Spanish Peaks, Colorado* (see Fig. 24)
43 *Longs Peak, Estes Park, Colorado* [no. 2]
44 *Evening, North Wales*
45 *Oberwesel on Rhine, Night*
46 *Spanish Peaks, Colorado* [no. 1]
47 *Mt. Evans, Colorado*
48 *Longs Peak from North Denver*
49 *Clear Creek from North Denver*
50 *Village of Gandria, Lake Lugano, Italy*
51 *Rome from Pincio Garden*
52 *Heidelberg, Sunset*
53 *Coast of North Wales*
54 *Florence from San Miniato* [no. 1]
68 *Arizona Clouds* [no. 1]
71 *Pikes Peak from Manitou*
74 *Mt. Byers, Colorado*
75 *Venetian Fishing Boats*
77 *Red Roofs of Siena*

2. Mountain Moods: The Estes Park Series

IN THE SPRING OF 1916, at his Denver studio-home at 1325 Logan Street, Burr held a memorable private showing of Estes Park scenes that he called Mountain Moods, and it remained a matter of local pride that their first public viewing took place the same year in "our Denver Art Gallery."[16] Series of watercolors or etchings, like those of Goya, Turner, Whistler, or Burr's contemporary John Taylor Arms, were not uncommon; but Mountain Moods was unique in that each of its sixteen scenes was rendered both in watercolor and as a black-and-white etching. The group consisted primarily of studies of pines. "Trees," wrote Edith W. Powell, "appeal not only to [Burr's] sense of the picturesque but to his imagination. They are for him one of Nature's most marvelous manifestations and he loves them best when they display the structure of their trunks and their branches. . . ."[17]

The *Rocky Mountain News* of April 2, 1916, commented that these were not so much pictorial views as they were expressions of "the spirit and feeling of the mountains captured by the genius of the artist. . . . Such a thing has never been attempted . . . , but the result is a fascinating group of impressions that should be preserved as a unit. . . . Mr. Burr's interesting . . . observations of nature's moods in the mountains is one of the most refreshing and delightful exhibits . . . shown this winter." The same paper reported on April 22, 1917, that the series, "done entirely for his own pleasure," had traveled to the Philadelphia Art Club and to Baltimore, receiving favorable notices in the eastern press.

Art magazines and newspapers began to carry reproductions of the etchings in Mountain Moods as early as 1916, and continued to do so through 1922 and 1923. (These are listed in Chapter VII.) The four used by Theodore Merrill Fisher (Nos. 161, 162, 168, 175) to illustrate an article on Burr would, he said, "bear out the contention that

---

16 *The Denver News,* Mar. 2, 1919.

17 "George Elmer [sic] Burr; an Etcher of the Desert," *The Print Connoisseur,* I (June 1921), 315. Among the sketches made by Burr in 1883 during a trip to South Bend, Ind. (see Chapter II under that year), the local paper cited "a sturdy oak with gnarled and exposed roots, . . . a slanting cedar . . . on the bank of the river [and a] wooded lane."

if this naturalist-etcher chose to confine his activity to this single type, his reputation for surpassing technique and distinction of subject would not suffer."[18] While interest in this set was still running high, Burr was already committed to a far more important and demanding project, the creation of his remarkable Desert Set.

The *Denver Times* of March 30, 1916, stated that there were twenty titles in Mountain Moods, and three days later the *Rocky Mountain News* reported fifteen. The final number seems to have been sixteen. Among those withdrawn was the popular *Sentinel Pine*, the etching of which (#135) reached an edition of two hundred. The watercolors in the series, none of which I have seen, were reportedly bought years ago by a Denver resident. The etchings, printed in editions that varied in number from plate to plate, could be bought singly.

A complete set of Mountain Moods etchings is now hanging on the west wall of the Special Collections Room in the Denver Public Library. Fogg Art Museum has at the moment all but two. The sixteen black-and-white etchings are:

159 *Broken Pine*
160 *Ragged Pine(s)*
161 *Brothers*
162 *Windswept Pine* [no. 3]
163 *Moraine Park* [no. 1]
164 *In Estes Park* [no. 1]
168 *The Leaning Pine*
169 *Longs Peak, Moonlight*
170 *Mt. Chapin, Estes Park* (see Fig. 25)
171 *Bent Pine, Estes Park*
172 *Solitary Pine*
173 *Longs Peak, Morning, Estes Park*
174 *Group of Pines, Estes Park*
175 *Black Canyon, Estes Park*
176 *Dead Pines, Estes Park*
177 *Skeleton Pine, Estes Park*

3. THE DESERT SET

IN MAY OF 1921, while he was still living in Denver, Burr finished the thirty-five plates, and copyrighted the last etchings, of the Desert Set. This series (which was sometimes referred to as Etchings of the Desert) was the more remarkable for having been wrought by a man always in delicate health — who, in fact, might never have undertaken the task had he not sought (possibly on his doctor's advice) to escape the rigors of the Colorado winters. These he habitually spent in New Mexico, Arizona, and California — mostly around Palm Springs, the Mojave Desert, and the Coachella Valley. Captivated by the distinctive beauties of these regions, he began a program of wandering at

---

[18] "George Elbert Burr," *The American Magazine of Art*, X (Feb. 1919), p. 127.

George Elbert Burr

Mt. Chapin. Estes Park.

FIGURE 25 — #170 *Mt. Chapin, Estes Park*   8½ x 6½ inches   Mountain Moods series

will, sketching and painting. His watercolors, which included desert scenes and a series of California gardens that attracted wide attention, found a ready market. But it was Burr's predilection for etching that led him to capture through the medium of the copper plate, and on a scale never before attempted, the lure of the West and Southwest — the changing moods, the tonal gradations and subtleties of daylight and darkness, the vast skies, the desert solitude and the exquisite detail of its flora and fleeting whirlwinds.

Burr had a good friend in Cyrus Boutwell, a prominent and enterprising art dealer whose shop was in Brinton Terrace, the attractive Bohemian art center that was also the artist's first home in Denver (see Fig. 13). It may have been at the insistence of this man, whose advice and opinions Burr had always respected, that the form of the Desert Set, unlike that of the earlier Mountain Moods series, was planned at its inception — at least to the extent that each etching was to be published in an edition of forty and numbered to show its sequence in the edition. This formidable task demanded much more than the pleasant but strenuous seeking out of Nature's scattered scenic treasures, and the infinitely patient and meticulous studio work that ensued. Burr was still using his old hand press that required considerable strength (see Fig. 17); he acquired a geared press only later, after moving to Phoenix (see Frontispiece). Also he did his own mounting, sold etchings at his studio, and supplied dealers throughout the country. The combination of physical exertion, inevitable and often uncongenial drudgery, restricted freedom, pressure exerted upon himself to fulfill the irksome assignment to which he was pledged, and, quite possibly, the clash of his independent spirit and artistic temperament with friendly and well-intentioned encounters with the dealer Boutwell and other interested persons — all this began to take its toll. Yet there was no voluntary slackening of Burr's innate creative drive, and even as he was approaching the limit of his endurance he sought, not rest, but merely a change as he again turned to the majestic scenery of Colorado. During 1922 and 1923 he finished and copyrighted, among others, three plates that were immediately in great demand: #226 *Pikes Peak, Colorado*, #228 *Timberline Storm*, and #230 *Old Pine, Estes Park, Colorado*. Each reached an edition of one hundred. (For locations of reproductions see Chapter VII.)

From 1920 on, the Denver newspapers mentioned his poor health with great frequency, and the *Rocky Mountain News* of June 24, 1923, reported that the artist and his wife had left for the home of his brother Linn in Cameron, Missouri, and that "Mr. Burr plans a complete rest, after a very active winter's work, and especially as he has a disabled arm, which has probably been overtaxed in his profession." Within two months they returned to Denver where he resumed work only to find that poor health was an obstacle. Frequent sojourns away from Denver helped him. He spent the winter of 1923-24 in Phoenix, but not in

FIGURE 26 — #194 *A Mirage* [no. 1]   7 x 10 inches   Desert Set

idleness, for he enjoyed his customary excursions over the countryside, and by the following spring had completed a number of pastels (see Fig. 29).[19] This afforded, in all probability, a considerable degree of therapeutic pleasure and relaxation; but the more strenuous and demanding work that he loved was beyond his endurance. In September 1924, having been advised by his doctor to move permanently to a more favorable climate, Burr sold the Logan Street house to the Denver Woman's Press Club and went to Phoenix, never to return.[20]

Independent once more and freed from all pressures, Burr gave no thought to retirement though he had now reached the age of sixty-five. He would never again take on the yoke of another etched series, though oblique hints that he might do so persisted;[21] yet such was his devotion to art that he was to complete approximately one hundred forty additional plates including many desert subjects, among them another mirage (#287) and two whirlwinds (#281 and #312). It has been said that Burr did some of his best work during this late period.

His reputation by no means waited upon the advent of the Desert Set, for he was well known to people of taste not only in the West and Southwest, but throughout the country, and his etchings had been exhibited in England and on the Continent. At the same time, his singleness of purpose contributed to a certain vagueness of personal identity in the competitive world of art; younger generations could find out little about him, and he did nothing to enlighten them. He belonged, in short, to that breed of artist who, shunning publicity and any display of aggressiveness or vanity, is content to let his work stand or fall on its merits alone. But the Desert Set provided the very "handle" that interested people had needed, and his splendid success quickly established him as the "Etcher of the Desert."

The series received instantaneous and universal acclaim. Three months after its completion, Lena M. McCauley, art editor of the *Chicago Evening Post,* hailed it in a feature article as "beyond question a monumental achievement of national importance . . . the greatest work in black and white of the present generation."[22] Hugh Walpole, who, as has been mentioned, spent several hours with Burr in the

---

[19] Eight of these, among the twenty or so owned by the Denver Public Library, bear dates between April 13 and 29, some showing that he made two in one day. Judging from the similarity of subject matter, others that are undated were possibly done at this time.

[20] That Burr was constantly on familiar terms with hard work leading to the point of exhaustion is shown as early as 1914, in his letter of September 6 addressed to the Denver artist Elizabeth Spalding; he warns her: ". . . don't try to do too much. Keep your health, I know what it means to work too many hours a day. One will break down, and then!" And four years after he moves to Phoenix he writes on January 10, 1928, to his friend Dr. Fosdick Jones, ". . . I know how you love your work, and like myself, work at it 'till exhausted."

[21] For example, both Allhusen, in his *George Elbert Burr, Etcher,* p. [8], and Leila Mechlin, in "New Plates by George Elbert Burr," *The American Magazine of Art,* XX (June 1929), 330, speak of the "First Desert Set."

[22] Aug. 16, 1921, "Mr. Burr's Etchings of National Import," in sect. "News of the Art World."

Logan Street studio, later remarked to Boutwell: "If a choice can be made among the many styles and subjects Mr. Burr has given the world, I am sure I'm most fond of what is called his 'Desert Set.' . . . I was amazed at his western delineations."[23] Will Simmons of Connecticut, a noted etcher and author, held that this series "has placed [Burr] definitely on the roster of American Art" and in a very distinctive way, for his prints "stand out . . . as some of the most personal, . . . most inherently American contributions to Etching up to date."[24] To Arthur Millier, Burr was "above everything else the etcher of the Great American Desert,"[25] and the New York Public Library, apropos of a large gift of Burr etchings on exhibit there from March 23 to May 4, 1936, called particular attention to those in the Desert Set.[26] The Grand Rapids Art Gallery exhibits the complete Desert Set once a year so that art students may study the technique and processes involved.

Allhusen, citing #194 *A Mirage* [no. 1] as an example (see Fig. 26), complimented Burr for rising above mere technical perfection to produce a "print that has to be seen to be believed," with a veracity "which one would not have thought possible to express in black and white."[27] In order to render so justly the divers subjects and moods depicted in this series, Burr used pure etching, drypoint, aquatint, soft ground, and mezzotint, often in combination. " 'I feel each thing in a different method,' to quote the artist."[28] The etchings were pulled either in black and white or in a single color of ink, e.g., pale gray, green, reddish orange, dark greenish blue, and shades of brown. Paper varied in color also, ranging from white and cream to pale shades of yellow, green, and pink. A very few copies of Nos. 189, 200, 214, and 222 were made as color etchings as part of their editions of forty. In size, the etchings in a complete series measure from 5 x 7 to 10 x 12 inches.

The Desert Set was widely exhibited again and again, sometimes as a one-man show, sometimes not. Its original price of $750 (averaging $18.75 per etching) soon rose to $1,200, but sales did not lag: on November 10, 1926, Burr reported to the Macbeth Gallery in New York, "My set of Desert prints of thirty-five subjects were all sold but four sets some time ago. They have gone around the world."

Early announcements had stated that thirty of the intended edition of forty sets would be offered intact — which presumably meant that each of the thirty-five etchings in a given set would bear an identical

23 *Rocky Mountain News*, Apr. 13, 1923.

24 "George Elbert Burr, Etcher of the American Desert," *The Print Connoisseur*, X (Oct. 1930), 257.

25 Introduction to *George Elbert Burr*, American Etchers series, Vol. VII (New York & London, [1930]), p. [1].

26 *Bulletin of the New York Public Library*, XL (Mar. 1936), 282.

27 Op. cit., pp. [10, 11].

28 *Bulletin*, loc. cit.

sequential number such as 5/40. That a considerably smaller block of matched sets was sold is suggested by the number of partial or "complete" sets scattered over the United States that have mixed numbers, and gaps supplied by one or more trial proofs. There are at least two plausible explanations of these broken sets. Some collectors insisted on having trial proofs, believing them to be more desirable because of their rarity; and Burr's disposition was such that he would have been the first to break into a set in order to sell one etching to someone eager to have it — and certain singles did indeed prove to be so popular that there was a lively demand for them. For whatever reason, so many sets were finally broken that today the assembling of a complete series even with mixed numbers would be extremely difficult, and, with matching numbers, well-nigh impossible.

Burr's consistent numbering of each impression (as 17/40, etc.) was a fortunate exception to his casual attitude toward the recording of tedious but helpful data, for in the case of an etching that is inscribed with only the artist's signature, the conventional abbreviations "del. et imp.," and the number "40," the latter identifies it immediately as one of the Desert Set, no edition of his other etchings having run to this number. Burr wrote titles on some impressions, many of which have variant wording. (For alternate titles see Chapter V.)

Trial proofs in the Desert Set cannot for the most part be readily identified by a person unfamiliar with the series. They rarely bear the number "40" or, for that matter, a title; and although one may occasionally come across the designation "Trial Proof No. 2," etc., it is impossible to say in general how many states the plate went through. An etching that has no title or other clue may be identified by comparing it in detail with the descriptions provided in Chapter VI.

It will be noted that the catalogue numbers assigned to the Desert Set, instead of being consecutive, are interrupted by #185 *Near Gallup,* #188 *Joshua Trees,* #204 *Ocotillo* [no. 1], #209 *Black Mesa,* and #219 *Death Valley.* All may at one time have been considered for inclusion; a trial proof of #188 (in the New York Public Library) has the notation in Burr's handwriting "Plate destroyed, no prints," and I have been unable to find copies of the other four in this group.

Fogg Art Museum has a superb and unique Desert Set, each of the thirty-five etchings being numbered 1/40. Among other complete sets found in various public collections, that of the Metropolitan Museum is noteworthy for its remarkably clear and brilliant trial proofs (probably "artist's proofs").

The etchings that comprise the Desert Set are:

184   *Arizona Clouds* [no. 2]
186   *Yuccas*
187   *Desert Night*
189   *Sandstorm on the Little Colorado River*

FIGURE 27 — #210 *Navajo Church, New Mexico* 7 x 5 inches Desert Set

IV

Numerical List
Types and Dimensions

NUMBERING SYSTEM. The numbers assigned to items 1-314 agree substantially with those in *The Print Connoisseur* "Catalogue Raisonné" and with the list in the American Etchers series, Volume VII, devoted to Burr. The former, published in January 1923, omits six in its list of 225 representing something less than two-thirds of the artist's total output. The latter, published in 1930, more or less repeats this list and continues it through #314 — about five-sixths of the total at the time of Burr's death nine years later. Both catalogues presumably used numbers supplied by Burr, and both omit #183. I have taken numbers 315-356 from Burr's holograph list now in the New York Public Library. Numbers 357-367, not assigned by Burr, are given to etchings that may be considered experimental; they were pulled in small numbers with the exception of #367 *Evening, Arizona*, printed privately for the associate members of the Brooklyn Society of Etchers.

TITLES. Approximately sixty percent of Burr's etchings are discovered to have one or more alternate titles, which sometimes vary only slightly (e.g., #213 *Cloudburst* and *Cloudburst, Arizona*), while others are totally dissimilar (e.g., #214 *From Indio, California* and *Morning Mist*). Burr, no stickler for consistency in penciled legends, used most of these titles interchangeably at one time or another, hence all so used must pass for correct. This means that any list of etching titles will inevitably include some arbitrary choices, while excluding other titles that may be equally familiar. For titles not found among those listed in the present catalogue, consult Chapter V.

A certain number of titles have now and then been devised as expedients by cataloguers and writers with only a superficial acquaintance with Burr's etchings — and there are even a very few impressions that Burr himself inadvertently mistitled. The latter are retained as matters of interest; but the others have been ruled out as legitimate titles, and omitted from the list of alternates in Chapter V.

Descriptive, rather than actual, titles are enclosed in brackets (e.g., #358 [Examples of Intaglio Processes]).

Bracketed numbers affixed to some titles (e.g., #287 A Mirage, Arizona [no. 2]) will alert the reader to the existence of other etchings having similar or identical titles or subjects. These listings with appended numbers should be used in conjunction with the descriptions in Chapter VI in order to detect subtle differences that have often resulted in the incorrect numbering or titling of etchings in public and private collections, and in reproductions. Any affixed number that forms part of Burr's own title (e.g., #326 Winter No. 2; #331 Palm Canyon Plate 2) is not enclosed in brackets.

DIMENSIONS, in inches, are taken from the plate marks. *The vertical measurement is given first, then the horizontal.* Many of the dimensions listed in the catalogue of *The Print Connoisseur,* and more than fifty in that of the American Etchers series, are either transposed or erroneous. These have been corrected insofar as possible. Discrepancies of 1/4 inch or less were not deemed important enough to record, since shrinkage of damped paper after printing is not uniform. I have retained from the aforementioned catalogues a certain number of unverified measurements. These, designated in each case by an asterisk, should be accepted with caution.

Abbreviations following titles designate TYPES[1] as follows: E (etching), D (drypoint), S (soft ground), A (aquatint), M (mezzotint), C (color). The label "color" (denoting etchings done in oils, *not* those printed in various-colored inks) merely directs attention to this noteworthy process; it has no bearing on the ratio of prints pulled in color and in black and white from the same plate.

1	*Old Cabins, Virginia* (E)	5 x 7
2	*Birch Trees* (E)	8 x 10
3	*The Campagna* (E)	5 x 8*
4	*Venice* (A)	9 x 12*

---

[1] I have relied largely on the earlier published catalogues for these data, which I assume to be fairly accurate although six color etchings are not so listed in the American Etchers series. In many cases these designations must not be considered absolute; Burr frequently achieved special and often subtle effects by combining several techniques on a single plate.

5	*Yarmouth, N.S.* (A)	4 x	5*
6	*Florence* [no. 1] (E)	7 x	10*
7	*Isolabona, Italy* (E)	5⅝ x	4
		6 x	4*
8	*Coast of Wales* (E)	7 x	10*
9	*Colorado River* (E)	5 x	8*
10	*Della Salute* (E)	5¾ x	4¼
		7 x	10*
11	*Mountain Home* (E)	8 x	6½*
12	*Near Lamy* [no. 1] (E)	5 x	7*
13	*Near Windsor* (E)	7 x	10*
14	*16th Street, Denver* (E)	11¼ x	5¼
		11 x	8*
15	*Study of Pines* [no. 1] (E)	2⅜ x	2⅞
16	*Study of Pines* [no. 2] (E)	3 x	2¾
17	*Study of Pines* [no. 3] (E)	2¼ x	3
18	*Study of Pines* [no. 4] (E)	3½ x	2
19	*Study of Pines* [no. 5] (E)	3 x	2
20	*Study of Pines* [no. 6] (E)	3½ x	2⅞
		3 x	2¼*
21	*Study of Pines* [no. 7] (E)	2½ x	2⅞
		2 x	3½*
22	*Cornfield* (E)	2 x	3½
		2½ x	3*
23	*Horseshoe Park* (E)	1⅞ x	4¼
24	*Longs Peak* [no. 1] (E)	1½ x	5
25	*Venetian Boats* (E)	2½ x	3
26	*Brook in Snow* (D)	8⅞ x	6½
		3½ x	2½
27	*Windswept Pine* [no. 1] (E)	1⅞ x	2⅝
28	*Low Tide, Abersoch* [no. 1] (E)	4½ x	7½*
29	*Rhine at Bacharach* (E)	5 x	7*
30	*Rhine below Rheinstein* (S)	5 x	8*
31	*Rhine at Pfalz* (E)	6 x	8*
32	*Rhine at Mouse Tower* (E)	5 x	8*
33	*Rhine at Oberwesel* (E)	5 x	8*
34	*The Rhine at Marksburg* (E)	6 x	8*
35	*Rhine at Katzenelnbogen* (E,A)	8 x	5
36	*Rhine at Drachenfels* (E)	5 x	8*
37	*Rhine at Niederlahnstein* (E)	6 x	8*
38	*Rome from Palatine Hill* (C,E,A)	6⅛ x	9⅜
39	*Florence from Monte Oliveto* [no. 1] (C,E,A)	6⅛ x	9⅜
40	*Rheinstein Castle* (C,E,A)	9⅜ x	6⅛
41	*Marksburg Castle* (C,E,A)	6⅛ x	9⅜
42	*Piñon Trees and Spanish Peaks, Colorado* (C,E,A)	6⅛ x	9⅜
43	*Longs Peak, Estes Park, Colorado* [no. 2] (C,E,A)	6⅛ x	9⅜

44	*Evening, North Wales* (C,A,S)	6⅛ x 9⅜
45	*Oberwesel on Rhine, Night* (C,E,A)	6⅛ x 9⅜
46	*Spanish Peaks, Colorado* [no. 1] (C,E,A,)	6¾ x 9¾
47	*Mt. Evans, Colorado* (C,E)	6¾ x 9¾
48	*Longs Peak from North Denver* (C,E,A)	7 x 10
49	*Clear Creek from North Denver* (C,E,A)	7 x 10
50	*Village of Gandria, Lake Lugano, Italy* (C,E,A)	5 x 8
51	*Rome from Pincio Garden* (C,E)	7 x 10
52	*Heidelberg, Sunset* (C,E,A)	6⅛ x 9⅜
53	*Coast of North Wales* (C,E,A)	6⅛ x 9⅜
54	*Florence from San Miniato* [no. 1] (C,E,A)	7 x 10
55	*Street in Sierre, Suisse* (E)	4¾ x 2¾
		3¾ x 2⅜
56	*Italian Village near Mentone* (E)	4½ x 5½*
57	*An Archway, Bordighera* (E)	4¾ x 3
58	*Brown Palace Hotel, Denver* (E)	6⅛ x 9⅜*
59	*Old Cedar and Pikes Peak* (E)	11½ x 9½
60	*Old Houses near Monte Carlo* (E)	3½ x 3½
61	*First Snow* [no. 1] (D)	3½ x 3½
62	*Winter* [no. 1] (D)	7 x 10
63	*Pity's at the Pool* [nude] (D)	10 x 12
64	*On the Little Colorado River, Arizona* (E)	5 x 7
65	*Near Ash Fork, Arizona* (E)	5 x 7
66	*A New England Road* [no. 1] (D)	7 x 10
67	*Florence from San Miniato* [no. 2] (D)	7 x 10
68	*Arizona Clouds* [no. 1] (C,M)	7 x 10
69	*St. Saphorin, Lake Geneva* (E)	6⅛ x 9⅜
		5½ x 7⅞
70	*Near Chavez, New Mexico* (E)	5 x 8
71	*Pikes Peak from Manitou* (C,E,A)	7 x 10
72	*The Fairy Glen, Bettws-y-coed, North Wales* (D)	8 x 5
73	*The Willows* (D)	7¾ x 5
74	*Mt. Byers, Colorado* (C,E,A)	7 x 10
75	*Venetian Fishing Boats* (C,E,A)	12 x 10
76	*Street in San Remo* (E)	10 x 7
77	*Red Roofs of Siena* (C,E)	7 x 10
78	*Stunted Cedars* (E)	7 x 10*
		5 x 8*
79	*Charcoal Boat, Venice* [no. 1] (E)	5 x 8*
80	*Windsor Castle, Evening* (E)	7 x 10
81	*Oaks in Winter* [no. 1] (D)	10 x 7
82	*High Street, Oxford* (E)	10 x 12
83	*Evening, Lake Geneva* (C,S)	12 x 10
84	*Warwick Castle, Night* (C,E,A)	7 x 10
85	*Elms, Windsor* (C,E)	7 x 10
86	*Temple of the Sibyl, Tivoli* (E)	10 x 7

FIGURE 28 — #212 *Grand Canyon* [no. 1]   12 x 10 inches   Desert Set

FIGURE 29 – *The Painted Desert, Arizona*   10¼ x 13¾ inches   Pastel

128	*Walpurgiskapelle, Nürnberg* (E)	7	x	5½
129	*Henkersteg, Nürnberg* (E)	5½	x	7
130	*Insel Schütt, Nürnberg* (E)	5½	x	7
131	*Windswept Spruces* (E)	7	x	5½
132	*Home of the Winds* [no. 1] (E)	5½	x	7
133	*Timberline Pine* (E)	5½	x	7
134	*Old Haw Trees* (S)	7	x	10
135	*Sentinel Pine* (E)	10	x	7
136	*Winter Evening* (E,A)	10	x	7
137	*Winter Morning* (E)	10	x	12
138	*Spanish Peaks* [no. 2] (C,E,A)	10	x	12
139	*Home of the Winds* [no. 2] (C,S)	10	x	12
140	*Old Cottonwoods* [no. 2] (E,A)	10	x	12
141	*Marblehead, Fisherman's Home* (E)	3	x	5
142	*Chimney Rock* (E)	3½	x	2
143	*The Range from Denver* (E)	3	x	5
144	*The Rhine at Laufenburg* (S)	3¾	x	5
145	*The Nightingale* [nude] (E,D)	8	x	5
146	*Cornfield in Winter* (D)	3½	x	6
147	*Warwick Castle from the Bridge* (E)	6	x	8
148	*Winter Snow* (D)	3⅝	x	3⅝
149	*Brook in Winter* [no. 1] (D)	3½	x	3½
150	*Old Oaks* (E)	10	x	7
		8	x	6
151	*Snow* (D)	3½	x	3½
152	*December* (D)	3½	x	3½
		3½	x	6*
153	*March Snow* (D)	5½	x	3½
154	*Black Pool* (D)	5½	x	3½
155	*The Range from Longmont, Colorado* (E,A)	1¾	x	7
156	*Longs Peak, Estes Park* [no. 3] (E,A)	1½	x	5
157	*Evening Cloud* [no. 1] (E,A)	3	x	5
		2	x	3½
158	*Autumn* [no. 2] (E,A)	2	x	3½*
159	*Broken Pine* (E,A)	9½	x	7½
160	*Ragged Pine(s)* (E)	9¾	x	7½
161	*Brothers* (E)	9¾	x	7½
162	*Windswept Pine* [no. 3] (E)	7½	x	9¾
163	*Moraine Park* [no. 1] (E)	9¾	x	7½
164	*In Estes Park* [no. 1] (E)	10	x	7
165	*Windy Hill No. 6* (E)	5½	x	3½
		4¾	x	3⅛
166	*Windy Hill No. 7* (E)	5½	x	3½
		3¾	x	3½
167	*Clear Creek Meadows, Denver* [no. 2] (E,A)	4	x	7*
168	*The Leaning Pine* (E)	8½	x	6½

169	*Longs Peak, Moonlight* (E,A)	6½ x 8½
170	*Mt. Chapin, Estes Park* (E,A)	8½ x 6½
171	*Bent Pine, Estes Park* (E)	8½ x 6½
172	*Solitary Pine* (E)	8½ x 6½
173	*Longs Peak, Morning, Estes Park* (E,A)	6½ x 8½
174	*Group of Pines, Estes Park* (E)	8½ x 6½
175	*Black Canyon, Estes Park* (E,A)	8½ x 6½
176	*Dead Pines, Estes Park* (E)	8½ x 6½
177	*Skeleton Pine, Estes Park* (E)	8½ x 6½
178	*Snow Storm, Estes Park* (E)	6 x 7
179	*The Pine and the Cloud, Estes Park* (E,D)	7 x 6
180	*Pines in Wind, Estes Park* (E)	6 x 7
181	*Moraine Park, Estes Park, Colorado* [no. 2] (E)	5 x 3½
182	*Rhône Valley* (E,A)	3 x 4
183	*[blank; see this number in Chapter VI]*	
184	*Arizona Clouds* [no. 2] (M)	7 x 10
185	*Near Gallup* (E)	3 x 5*
186	*Yuccas* (D)	7 x 4½
		6¾ x 5
		6¾ x 4½
		7¾ x 4½*
187	*Desert Night* (A)	9¾ x 7½
188	*Joshua Trees* (E)	7 x 5
		8 x 5*
189	*Sandstorm on the Little Colorado River* (C,S)	6¾ x 9¾
190	*Near Kingman, Arizona* (S)	6¼ x 9½
191	*Soapweed* [no. 1] (D)	7 x 5
192	*Palm Canyon* [no. 1] (D)	7 x 5
193	*Santa Catalina Mountains, Tucson, Arizona* (D)	5 x 8
194	*A Mirage* [no. 1] (D)	7 x 10
195	*Oasis of Seven Palms, California* (D)	5 x 7
196	*Drifting Sand near Amboy, California* (D)	6 x 7
197	*Whirlwinds, Mojave Desert* [no. 1] (D)	5 x 7
198	*Prickly Pear Cactus* (D)	7¼ x 5
199	*Desert Dunes* [no. 1] (D)	5 x 7
200	*Cholla Cactus* (C,D)	8 x 5
201	*Palo Verde Trees* (S)	5 x 7
202	*Palm Springs, California* (D)	5¼ x 7
203	*Twilight, Laguna, New Mexico* [no. 2] (A)	5 x 8
204	*Ocotillo* [no. 1] (E)	8 x 5*
205	*Barrel Cactus* [no. 1] (D)	5 x 8
206	*Giant Cactus* (D)	8 x 6
207	*Near Lamy, New Mexico* [no. 2] (S)	10 x 7
208	*Moonlight, Holbrook, Arizona* (A)	5 x 8
209	*Black Mesa* (D)	4 x 6*
210	*Navajo Church, New Mexico* (D)	7 x 5

211	*Needles Mountains, Colorado River, Arizona* (D)	9½ x 12
212	*Grand Canyon* [no. 1] (S)	12 x 10
213	*Cloudburst* (S)	10 x 12
214	*From Indio, California* (C,S,A)	10 x 12
215	*Evening Cloud* [no. 2] (S,A)	12 x 10
216	*Mesa Encantada, New Mexico* [no. 1] (E)	6 x 8
217	*Piñon Trees* (E)	10 x 12
218	*Old Cedars, New Mexico* (E)	10 x 12
219	*Death Valley* (E)	5 x 8*
220	*Desert Shower* (E,D)	7 x 10
221	*Sunset* (E)	7 x 10
222	*San Francisco Mountains, Arizona* [no. 1] (C,S)	7 x 10
223	*Dawn in the Land of the Buttes* (E)	6 x 8
224	*November* (E)	7½ x 6
225	*Brook in Winter* [no. 2] (E,A)	7½ x 6
226	*Pikes Peak, Colorado* (E)	12 x 10
227	*Old Cedars and Spanish Peaks, Colorado* (E)	10 x 12
228	*Timberline Storm* (E,S)	10 x 12
229	*Bear Creek Canyon, Denver, Colorado* (E)	12 x 10
230	*Old Pine, Estes Park, Colorado* (E)	12 x 10
231	*Village Street, Lake Lugano, Italy* [no. 1] (E)	12 x 10
232	*Old Pines near Timberline* (E)	8½ x 6½
233	*Old Pine and Cedar* (E)	9¾ x 7⅞
234	*Near Monterey* (E)	3½ x 5
235	*Old Cypress near Monterey* (E,A)	5 x 3½
236	*[Christmas Plate]* [no. 1] (E)	3½ x 5
237	*[Christmas Plate]* [no. 2] (E)	3½ x 5
238	*Road in the Campagna, Rome* (D)	5 x 7
239	*Mouth of the Arno* (D)	6 x 9
240	*Ventimiglia, Italy* (D)	7 x 10
241	*Florence from Fiesole* (E,D)	5¾ x 9
242	*Florence from Monte Oliveto* [no. 2] (E)	12 x 10
243	*Bordighera, Italy* (E)	7 x 10*
244	*Rome from Tivoli* (D)	7 x 10
245	*Capri from Sorrento* (A)	10 x 7
246	*Venice after Storm* (E,D)	10 x 12
247	*From French Academy, Rome* (D)	5 x 8
248	*From Appian Way, Rome* (D)	6 x 9
		5 x 8*
249	*Old Olive and Monte Carlo* (D)	10 x 12
250	*Superstition Mountain, Apache Trail, Arizona* [no. 1] (E)	7 x 10
251	*Near Echo Canyon, Phoenix, Arizona* (E)	10 x 7
252	*Indian Homes, Gila River, Arizona* (E)	5 x 7
253	*Road to Paradise Valley, Arizona* (E)	5¼ x 7¼
254	*Arizona Canal, Phoenix* (E)	6 x 9
255	*Camelback Mountain, Phoenix, Arizona* (E)	7 x 10

FIGURE 30 — #10 *Della Salute*   5¾ x 4¼ inches

Courtesy of the Fogg Art Museum, Harvard University, gift of the Misses Margaret and Mary Edson, 1935

256	*Arizona Storm* (D)	4½ x	6
257	*The Little Canyon* (E)	6 x	4½
258	*Storm in the Painted Desert, Arizona* (D)	4½ x	6
259	*San Xavier Mission, Tucson, Arizona* (E)	7 x	10
260	*Storm on the Little Colorado River, Arizona* (D)	4½ x	6
261	*Estrella Mountains, Gila River, Arizona* (E)	5 x	7
262	*The Desert, Arizona* [no. 2] (E,S,D)	6 x	8
263	*Desert Sentinels, Apache Trail, Arizona* (E)	5 x	7½
264	*Fish Creek, Apache Trail, Arizona* (E)	6⅝ x	4⅞
		6⅝ x	4
265	*Summer Cloud, Apache Trail, Arizona* (D)	8 x	10
		10 x	12*
266	*Moonlight, Phoenix, Arizona* (E,A)	3½ x	5⅜
		3½ x	5
267	*A New England Road* [no. 2] (D)	5 x	8
268	*Cloud Shadows, Apache Trail, Arizona* (D)	8 x	10
269	*Evening, Painted Desert, Arizona* (D)	5 x	7
270	*First Snow* [no. 2] (D)	3½ x	3½
271	*Oaks in Winter* [no. 2] (D)	9 x	7
272	*Pyramid Mountain, New Mexico* (D)	2⅝ x	4⅝
273	*Brook in Winter No. 3* (D)	10 x	8
274	*Evening, Apache Trail, Arizona* (E,D)	5 x	7
275	*Canyon Rim, Arizona* (D)	10 x	8
276	*Misty Day, Pauls Wharf, London* (D)	10 x	8
277	*Coast at Monterey, California* (E)	10 x	8
278	*Eucalyptus Trees, Santa Barbara* (D)	10 x	7
279	*Old Charcoal Boat, Venice* [no. 3] (E)	5 x	8
280	*Misty Moonlight, Estes Park, Colorado* (E,A)	10 x	7
281	*Whirlwinds, Dead Mountains, Mojave Desert, California* [no. 2] (D)	8 x	10
282	*Evening, Paradise Valley, Arizona* (D)	8 x	10
283	*Springtime, Paradise Valley, Arizona* (D)	12 x	10
284	*The Edge of the Desert, Arizona* (E,D)	10 x	12
285	*On Lake Lugano, Italy* [no. 2] (E)	10 x	7
286	*Soapweed, Arizona* [no. 2] (E,D)	10 x	7
287	*A Mirage, Arizona* [no. 2] (D)	8 x	10
288	*Barrel Cactus* [no. 2] (D)	7 x	5
289	*Ocotillo, Arizona* [no. 2] (E,D)	8 x	5
290	*Nest of the Desert Wren, Arizona* (D)	8 x	5
291	*"Cucumber" Cactus, Arizona* (D)	7 x	5
292	*Indian Home, Salt River Mountains, Arizona* (D)	8 x	10
293	*Evening, Navajo Country, Arizona* (D)	10 x	12
294	*Indian Homes, Apache Reservation, Arizona* (D)	8 x	10
295	*Road to Apache Reservation, Arizona* (D)	10 x	8
296	*In Estes Park, Colorado* [no. 2] (D)	10 x	8
297	*Woods in Winter* (D)	10 x	8

298	*Sketch on Apache Trail, Arizona* (E)	7	x	5
299	*Hassayampa River, Arizona* (D)	5	x	7
300	*The Etcher* (D)	7	x	5
301	*Twilight, New Mexico* [no. 3] (E)	5	x	7*
302	*Youth and Age* (D)	10	x	8*
303	*Arizona Sunshine* [nude] (D)	10	x	8
304	*Palo Verde* [nude] (D)	5	x	7
305	*Desert Poppies* [nude] (D)	5	x	7
306	*Sand Dunes* [nude] (D)	6	x	8
		4¾	x	6¾
307	*New Moon* [nude] (D)	5	x	7
308	*Yuccas* [nude] (D)	8	x	10
309	*Apache Maid* [nude] (D)	8	x	10
310	*Old Cedar* [nude] (D)	8	x	10
311	*Dawn* [nude] (D)	10	x	8
312	*Whirlwinds* [no. 3] (D)	8	x	10
313	*Solitude* (D)	8	x	10*
314	*Arizona Night* (E,A)	8	x	10
315	*Near Needles, Arizona* (E,D)	8	x	10
		7	x	9
316	*Valley of the Lledr, Wales* [no. 2] (D)	5	x	8
317	*Old Cedar, Ash Fork, Arizona* (E,D)	10	x	12
318	*Desert Twilight* (E)	5	x	6¾
319	*Paradise Valley, Arizona* (E,D)	5	x	8
320	*Mesa Encantada, New Mexico* [no. 2] (E,D)	4¾	x	8
321	*Palm Canyon near Palm Springs* [no. 3] (E,D)	7	x	5
322	*Verde River, Apache Reservation, Arizona* (E,D)	8	x	10
323	*Dunes near Palm Springs, California* [no. 2] (E,D)	5	x	7
324	*The Land of Mystery — The Desert* (E,D)	7	x	9½
325	*Superstition Mountain, Apache Trail, Arizona, Night* [no. 2] (D)	12	x	10
326	*Winter No. 2* (D)	7	x	10
327	*Road to Bear Lake* (E,D)	10	x	8
328	*Longs Peak, Estes Park, Colorado* [no. 4] (E,D)	9¾	x	7¾
329	*New Moon and Morning Star, Phoenix, Arizona* (E,D,A)	10	x	8
330	*Grand Canyon Plate 3* (E,D)	10	x	8
331	*Palm Canyon Plate 2* (D)	10	x	8
332	*Spanish Peaks, Colorado* [no. 3] (E,D)	8	x	10
333	*Desert Clouds* (E,D)	11¾	x	10
334	*Evening on the Little Colorado River* (E,D)	10	x	12
335	*Desert Monuments, Arizona* (E,D)	10	x	12
336	*San Gorgonio from the Coachella Valley, California* (E,D)	8	x	10
337	*Painted Cliffs, Apache Trail, Arizona* (E)	10	x	8
338	*Mountain of the Holy Cross* (E,D)	10	x	8
339	*San Francisco Peaks, Arizona* [no. 2] (E,D)	8	x	10
340	*Sketch in Taormina, Sicily* (D)	12	x	10
341	*Chimney Pots, Lausanne, Suisse*	....	x	....

342	*Old House in Wye Valley* (S)	8 x 10
343	*Harlech Castle, Wales* (D)	8 x 9¾
344	*Oberlahnstein, Rhine* (S)	8 x 10
345	*Sketch of Florence from San Miniato* [no. 3] (D)	8 x 9¾
346	*Florence from Monte Oliveto* [no. 3] (D)	7 x 9
347	*Valley at Toblach, Tyrol* (D)	7 x 9
348	*West Gate, Warwick* (S)	9 x 7
349	*Lake Lugano, Italy* [no. 3] (E,D)	10 x 7¼
350	*Stone Pines near Sorrento, Italy* (E,D)	12 x 10
351	*Iffley Mill near Oxford* (D)	10½ x 12¼
352	*Charcoal Boat, Venice* [no. 2] (D)	5 x 8
353	*Old Bridge, Chester, England* [no. 2] (D,S)	5 x 8
354	*Valley of the Llugwy, Wales* (S)	5 x 8
355	*Devil's Bridge near Lucca, Italy*	.... x ....
356	*Old Cedar near Kingman, Arizona* (D,A)	9½ x 7⅞
357	*Low Tide, North Wales* [no. 2] (D)	8 x 9¾
358	*[Examples of Intaglio Processes]*	2⅞ x 7
359	*Sketch in the Mojave Desert* (D)	3¼ x 6⅞
360	*Brook and Trees, Winter* (D)	6 x 3½
361	*Portrait of the Artist* (D)	6 x 4
362	*Indian Homes, Colorado River, Arizona* (E,S)	7½ x 11¾
363	*Near Our Cabin* (E)	5 x 8
364	*[My First Etching]* (E)	3 x 4½
365	*[My Second Attempt at Etching]* (E)	4½ x 3
366	*[Cactus Club Dinner Etching]* (E)	5½ x 2½
367	*Evening, Arizona* (E,D)	5 x 7

V

Alphabetical List
including Alternate Titles

MAIN TITLES (i.e., those listed in Chapters IV and VI) are here printed in italics to differentiate them from alternate titles, which are always in roman type. Titles in both categories (as explained in the previous chapter) may be considered correct except as noted.

Titles containing one or more minor but troublesome variants in wording are so numerous that the reader may discover an occasional example not accounted for in this chapter. To obviate multiple listings of such titles, any word or letter that may or may not appear is enclosed in parentheses. Thus entry #213 *Cloudburst (Arizona)* denotes the existence of two possible titles, *Cloudburst,* or *Cloudburst, Arizona;* and, to cite a more extreme case, #265 *(A) Summer Cloud(s) (Apache Trail) (Country) (Arizona)* can be identified by the words "A Summer Cloud," "Summer Cloud," or "Summer Clouds" — with or without one or more of the additional components "Apache Trail," "Country," and "Arizona."

George Elbert Burr

Figure 31 — #73 *The Willows*   7¾ x 5 inches

---

[1] Burr's parenthesis.

George Elbert Burr

Street in San Remo - Italy

Figure 32 — #76 *Street in San Remo*   10 x 7 inches

---

[2] Burr's spelling in this and the two titles following: "Oliveato."

---

[3] For remark on variant spellings see this listing in Chapter VI.

76

FIGURE 33 — #82 *High Street, Oxford*   10 x 12 inches

© George Albert Burr

FIGURE 34 — #125 *Catania Gate, Taormina, Sicily*   10 x 7 inches

---

[4] For remark on variant spellings see this listing in Chapter VI.

© George Elbert Burr

Old Cottonwoods   Denver

FIGURE 35 — #140 *Old Cottonwoods* [no. 2]   10 x 12 inches

VI

Catalogue Raisonné
of the Etchings

MAIN ENTRIES consist of three particulars — catalogue numbers, titles, and dimensions — that have been dealt with in the introduction to Chapter IV.

An entry is followed in most cases by descriptive details selected primarily to facilitate quick and accurate identification of the etching, and, especially, to avert confusion with others that depict similar subject matter. Exceptions are etchings (numbering ten percent of the total) that I have not found in major public and private collections here and abroad or as illustrations in books, periodicals, and newspapers, or located through numerous inquiries. It would appear that these elusive prints, a majority of which represent scenes sketched by Burr during his years abroad, have disappeared from public view not because they are in any way inferior to the artist's more familiar works, but because they were issued in small editions that passed quickly into private hands where they remain today. Descriptions of locales are supplied for this lesser group, where practicable, as a possible aid in identification.

It should be assumed that each impression bears the signature "George Elbert Burr" (or, very infrequently, "George E. Burr" — a first cousin in the East signed himself thus), written in pencil on the lower margin, to the left and just below the plate mark. (Two exceptions that I own, #17 and #69, are noted.) "Del. et Imp." often appears on this margin in the center or at the right, close to the plate mark.

Burr's handwritten titles (of irregular occurrence) were added in pencil, usually on the bottom margin directly beneath the plate mark, either in the center or at the right. In rare cases he wrote them at the left, on the extreme lower edge of the bottom margin. He sometimes penciled the catalogue number alone on the reverse of the etching itself. When the title and catalogue number are supplied by another hand, they usually appear on the lower margin of the etching where, when it is mounted, they are hidden under the window mat. They may occur also on the lower edge of the mount or on the face of the window mat.

Most of the etchings bear no numbers whatsoever. Exceptions are the color etchings, which often are given a sequential number only (e.g., No. 12); those in the Desert Set, which show both the sequential number and that of the total run (e.g., 26/40); and a few others that show, following a slash, the number in the edition (e.g., #276 *Misty Day, Pauls Wharf, London* /63). Trial proofs may or may not furnish useful data; some show the number, state, and even a title, while others bear only the words "trial proof" and the artist's signature. An etching that has nothing at all written on it may be either a trial proof or a finished print that the artist neglected to sign. I have no doubt that a rarity such as this was Burr's own work, since he and his wife scrupulously destroyed all copper plates with the exception of a few that were given to friends as keepsakes.

The purely descriptive paragraphs in the catalogue are often followed, in brackets, by further details about the etchings, and the locales that Burr visited and sketched. Additional technical data introduced by the words "My copy" provide a record of variations that should prove useful in identifying etchings that vary slightly from the familiar pattern, or that lack a title or other obvious clues.

Two classes of information occasionally written on etching mounts, but not dealt with here, call for a word of caution. Burr sometimes noted on a particular etching that another copy was to be found in a certain museum. This location was correct as written, but for various reasons it may not hold today. For example, a museum director may have chosen to part with one or more Burr etchings or even to eliminate an entire collection;[1] or, as already mentioned in the case of the Luxembourg (which is no longer a museum), acquisitions may have been moved as a whole or dispersed among several public institutions. A second caution applies to inscribed mounts that former owners may have inadvertently shifted from one etching to another, or blank mounts that someone lacking accurate information may have supplied with erroneous data such as an incorrect title or catalogue number.

---

[1] Records in my daybook, run two years apart at a certain museum in this country, show a discrepancy of twenty etchings in the total number there.

© George Elbert Burr

Figure 36 — #180 *Pines in Wind, Estes Park*   6 x 7 inches

As explained earlier, an entry that is labeled "color etching" as a mark of special interest may also have been printed in black and white, perhaps in a larger edition. Burr sent many etchings as Christmas cards (see #27 *Windswept Pine* [no. 1] and remark). Examples that I have seen will be noted. A glossary following the Appendix contains special terms and abbreviations used in this chapter. Books and periodical references cited in abridged form are included in the Selected Bibliography.

1   *Old Cabins, Virginia*   5 x 7
Cabins close together. Two chimneys. Washing on line l. Path from cabins to ctr. fgrd. with man r. facing away. A few trees. Birds in sky. "BURR" on plate lower l. No monogram. [Burr's note on NYPL copy identifies locale as Daggers Springs, Va., 1880.]

2   *Birch Trees*   8 x 10
White birches ctr., leaves indicated by scribbly lines, light sky beyond tree trunks. Fallen trees fgrd. l. and r. "BURR" on plate lower l. [Burr's note on NYPL copy: "Mackinaw (Island) interior, 1881. Only proof."]

3   *The Campagna*   5 x 8*
Have not found this etching. [The campagna is a flat coastal area in Italy about thirty miles wide and fifty miles long, lying along the Tyrrhenian Sea. It includes Rome, with Civitavecchia and Terracina as the approximate northern and southern boundaries.]

4   *Venice*   9 x 12*
Have not found this etching.

5   *Yarmouth, N.S.*   4 x 5*
Have not found this etching.

6   *Florence* [no. 1]   7 x 10*
Have not found this etching.

7   *Isolabona, Italy*   5⅝ x 4; 6 x 4*
Vertical interest in narrow portion of four- or five-story building on far side of narrow river. Archways, overhanging wooden balconies, windows, and roofs. Kneeling figure r. on near bank in fgrd. Fades to edges. Monogram r. [Isolabona, almost equidistant from Ventimiglia and Bordighera, is located in the Nervia Valley a few miles inland from Italian Riviera. Used by Burr as Christmas card, 1911.]

8   *Coast of Wales*   7 x 10*
Have not found this etching. [The coast of Wales offered the artist a variety of charming vistas: great stretches of flat beaches, rocky headlands, inlets and estuaries, rounded mtns., all in a great variety of atmospheric conditions.]

9   *Colorado River*   5 x 8*
Have not found this etching. [Burr was especially interested in the part of this great river that passes through Arizona or forms its boundary line.]

10 *Della Salute* 5¾ x 4¼; 7 x 10* (see Fig. 30)
White marble church, scrolled buttresses, two domes, and campanile. Steps leading down to water's edge. Gondola, two figures. Other small boats r. fgrd. Building with low, sloping roof beside church r. No monogram. See Fig. 57, a watercolor. [Santa Maria della Salute, dating from early seventeenth century, stands on the point of land where the Grand Canal meets the Canal della Giudecca.]

11 *Mountain Home* 8 x 6½*
Have not found this etching.

12 *Near Lamy* [no. 1] 5 x 7*
Have not found this etching. [Lamy is a small town a few miles south of Santa Fe, New Mexico.]

13 *Near Windsor* 7 x 10*
Have not found this etching. [The town, and the castle situated in a 1,500-acre park, are on the Thames approximately fifteen miles west of London.]

14 *16th Street, Denver* 11¼ x 5¼; 11 x 8*
Unusual measurements. Slender Daniels and Fisher Tower appears to be about fifteen stories high. Near top, four columns support three arches; above these, a clock and small dome surmounted by flag. Autos and pedestrians in fgrd. On sidewalk l. a clock on post. The Front Range of the Rockies forms bgrd. beyond building to l. Copyrighted 1915. No monogram. [This tower, said to have been inspired by the Campanile in St. Mark's Square, Venice, is still standing.]

15 *Study of Pines* [no. 1] 2⅜ x 2⅞
Four dark pines with white trunks in group ctr. to r., first on l. leaning r. into others. Dark mtns. form skyline. A few scattered rocks. Shadows to r. Sky filled with lines rising to upper r. Monogram l. of ctr. [Used by Burr as Christmas card, 1916.]

16 *Study of Pines* [no. 2] 3 x 2¾
Small group of ragged trees near timber line, close together l. of ctr., windblown to r. Horizontal lines on trunks make them appear rounded. Tangled branches. Clinging cones and clusters of leaves near trunks and to r. Mtn. with snow in bgrd. No monogram. This is probably #107 *Windswept, Estes Park* (q.v.), plate cut and reworked, third tree added on r.

17 *Study of Pines* [no. 3] 2¼ x 3
On l. a limber pine at tree line leaning far r., roots grabbing into rocks. Clumps of leaves in topmost branches. Skyline of white-clad mtns. r. on a line with lowest part of tree. Fine-lined streaks in sky upper l. to ctr. r. Reminds one of Japanese print. Monogram l. Artist's signature sometimes on r. [My copy: printed on stiff card; signature l. in pencil inside plate mark; no title. Used by Burr as Christmas card.]

18 *Study of Pines* [no. 4] 3½ x 2
Two partially dead pines with tops broken off, curved trunks, roots in rocks l. of ctr. Clusters of leaves clinging to branches in ctr. Pointed mtns. with snow beyond deep, dark valley. Monogram l. of ctr. [Used by Burr as Christmas card.]

19 *Study of Pines* [no. 5]   3 x 3; 3 x 2

Tall, slender pine, flat crown of branches, others drooping at midpoint of twisted trunk, roots in rocks lower r. Sharp mtn. peaks form skyline. Some snow. Larger size has vertical remarque (three separate nudes) at l. Smaller size becomes #19. Monogram lower r. [Arizona State University copy printed on upper half of 5¼ x 3⅝ sheet. At bottom margin: "George Elbert Burr. First State. Christmas Plate 1910 with figures."]

20 *Study of Pines* [no. 6]   3½ x 2⅞; 3 x 2¼*

High-altitude view with three tall, sharp-pointed trees l. of ctr. in fgrd., wind-blown branches to r., no branches on l. of trunks. Dark leaves, white trunks. White mtn. far distance r. Three or four birds in sky. Monogram l. Similar to #131 *Windswept Spruces* (q.v.). [Used by Burr as Christmas card.]

21 *Study of Pines* [no. 7]   2½ x 2⅞; 2 x 3½*

Gnarled, bare, windswept tree, roots in rocks r. Many forked branches, all swept toward l. Streaks from r. suggest rain or sleet. White mtn. with sharp peaks forms low horizon l. Monogram l. Skies in some are lines; others aquatint. [Used by Burr as Christmas card, 1918.]

22 *Cornfield*   2 x 3½; 2½ x 3*

Flat field with corn shocks, scattered pumpkins. House, farm buildings, trees far l. Low skyline of mtns. Many birds in sky r. of ctr. Monogram l. [Used by Burr as Christmas card, 1918.]

23 *Horseshoe Park*   1⅞ x 4¼

In fgrd. one of many curves made by Fall River as it meanders through flat meadow within Rocky Mountain National Park at elevation of over 8,500 feet. Dark tree l. on bank reflected in water. Three large, snow-spotted mtns. of the Mummy Range form bgrd. Ypsilon Mountain, its snowy crevices in star pattern, easily identified in ctr. Monogram r. [My copy: on stiff card; no title.]

24 *Longs Peak* [no. 1]   1½ x 5

Miniature landscape of mtns. Longs Peak and others in Rocky Mountain National Park, pure white and snow-covered, rising high and forming bgrd. Lesser peaks in middle distance are dark. Flat meadow crossed by stream bordered by occasional trees from middle distance to fgrd. Monogram r. With aquatint added, this becomes #156 *Longs Peak, Estes Park* [no. 3] (q.v.). Cf. also #155 *The Range from Longmont, Colorado*.

25 *Venetian Boats*   2½ x 3

Boat broadside with two small figures, two sails, in heavy drypoint and reflected in water l. of ctr. On r. a white church (San Giorgio Maggiore) with two domes, campanile, other buildings, small boats, all reflected in water. No monogram. [Used by Burr as Christmas card, 1919.]

26 *Brook in Snow*   8⅞ x 6½; 3½ x 2½

Miniature snow scene. On l., tall trees with many snow-laden branches stand within curve of dark brook; another curve of brook in distance ctr. Round trees r. in distance. Many fine horizontal lines in stream and in sky. Larger size has remarque which entirely surrounds small scene and is plain gray except for lower third where a group of wood nymphs with airy draperies is sketchily drawn

© George Elbert Burr

Trial proof - /40

Figure 37 — #197 *Whirlwinds, Mojave Desert* [no. 1]   5 x 7 inches   Desert Set

against a darker background. Monogram l. No monogram on small cut version. [Both sizes sent as Christmas cards. The figures in remarque resemble bas-relief mounted above fireplace in artist's Denver studio (see Fig. 16).]

27 *Windswept Pine* [no. 1]   1⅞ x 2⅝   (see title page)
A limber pine in Rockies near timber line with exposed talon-like roots, its trunk and all branches windswept l. Mtns. in l. distance with snow in ravines. Low skyline. Monogram r. [Burr's note on NYPL copy: "My first Christmas Card." Copy in Honolulu Academy of Arts bears the date 1915. Burr, during his lifetime, often sent etchings of various sizes as season's greetings. Some small etchings and drypoints were made expressly for Christmas cards. My copy: no title.]

28 *Low Tide, Abersoch* [no. 1]   4½ x 7½*
Have not found this etching. [Abersoch in North Wales is located on the Lleyn Peninsula at St. Tudwal's Road, Cardigan Bay.]

29 *Rhine at Bacharach*[2]   5 x 7*
Have not found this etching. [Bacharach is on l. bank between Bingen and Oberwesel. A little above the town and overlooking both it and the Rhine stand the romantic Gothic ruins of Wernerkapelle; the tall, arched windows and stone tracery, when seen silhouetted against the sky, stir one's imagination.]

30 *Rhine below Rheinstein*   5 x 8*
Have not found this etching. [American Etchers series lists as soft ground. On l. bank of Rhine between Bingen and Bacharach, Rheinstein Castle, built on edge of sheer cliffs, commands a view up and down river. Most pictures of the castle show tree on upstream side growing close to castle and cliff edge. When Burr was there in the early 1900s, vineyards were more extensive in the area than they are today.]

31 *Rhine at Pfalz*   6 x 8*
Have not found this etching. [Pfalz Castle, built in fourteenth century on rock midstream, is hexagonal in shape, with angle on upstream end sharp like prow of ship, to break up river ice. Made of reddish-colored stone with many small, sharply pointed gables and small towers all roofed in dark gray slate. A larger, hexagonal tower stands in ctr., its roof resembling World War I German officer's helmet. The town of Caub is on r. bank near-by, Gutenfels Castle on mountaintop above.]

32 *Rhine at Mouse Tower*   5 x 8*
Have not found this etching. [Der Mäuseturm, built on small reef in Binger Loch near busy town of Bingen just below where the Nahe flows into the Rhine, has distinctive tall, slender tower on upstream end. Tower is cream color with red trim. Opposite on r. bank part way up mtn. is thirteenth-century ruin of Ehrenfels, with two towers.]

33 *Rhine at Oberwesel*   5 x 8*
Have not found this etching. [For description of locale see #45 *Oberwesel on Rhine, Night*, a color etching.]

---

2 With only two exceptions (Drachenfels above Königswinter, and Laufenburg between Konstanz and Basel), Burr's Rhine subjects are located between Wiesbaden and Coblenz. Here the river travels past picturesque castles, ruins, and mountains descending sharply on both banks.

34 *The Rhine at Marksburg* 6 x 8*

Have not found this etching. [See #41 *Marksburg Castle,* a color etching.]

35 *Rhine at Katzenelnbogen* 8 x 5

On opposite (r.) bank of river some houses and a tower (St. Goarshausen) barely reflected in Rhine in fgrd. High above on solid rocks is fourteenth-century castle erected by Count Johann of Katzenellenbogen. Dark print. Monogram r. [Once called Neu-Katzellenbogen, the name contracted in time to Katzenelnbogen and Katzelnbogen and is now commonly called Burg Katz (Cat Castle) or "The Cat." Viewed from some angles the castle resembles a crouching cat facing the river, with ears (two small towers with pointed roofs), a fat body, and large tail.]

36 *Rhine at Drachenfels* 5 x 8*

Have not found this etching. [The crumbling ruins of Drachenfels, birthplace of Rhenish legends, overlook the Seven Mountains on r. bank above Königswinter, diagonally across the Rhine from Bonn. Extensive views in all directions.]

37 *Rhine at Niederlahnstein* 6 x 8*

Have not found this etching. [Small town just below junction of the Lahn and the Rhine. Situated in flat park near river and surrounded by trees is Johanneskirche zu Niederlahnstein, built in 1140 and later restored — a small stone church with groups of open arches on three high levels, square roof rising to a point. The Lahn flows on both sides of large rock that figures in town's name. Strikingly beautiful Stolzenfels Castle, built in thirteenth century, is across the river.]

38 *Rome from Palatine Hill* 6⅛ x 9⅜

Color etching. On r. a high ruined wall with row of straight poplars growing out of it silhouetted against sky. Rooftops l. A path r. of ctr., man walking away. St. Peter's and other domes dimly seen ctr. and l. in distance. Monogram l. [My copy: muted colors suggest antiquity; no title.]

39 *Florence from Monte Oliveto* [no. 1] 6⅛ x 9⅜

Color etching. Olive tree with forked trunk l., delicate leaves silhouetted against bgrd. of white buildings and sky. Olive grove (Ital. *oliveto*) in fgrd. on sloping mtn. Cathedral, Baptistry, and Campanile distinguishable among roofs. Hills beyond. Monogram l. Cf. #242 *Florence from Monte Oliveto* [no. 2], in black and white and a larger size. See also #346 *Florence from Monte Oliveto* [no. 3]. [Burr's note on Phoenix Art Museum copy: "My first successful color plate. Made and printed in Tom's (sic) River, N.J., 1904."]

40 *Rheinstein Castle* 9⅜ x 6⅛ (see Fig. 23)

Color etching; also pulled in black and white. High on rock, ctr., a crenelated castle; at extreme l. its small adjoining chapel with sharp spire; at r., castle's round tower with horizontal pole and small flag at end extending toward Rhine far below r. In ctr. a prominent, slender tree, its leafy top against sky. Shadows in rocks beneath castle vaguely suggest benign face of ancient river god looking down on Rhine. Monogram l. [My copy: color; No. 54; Del. et Imp.; no title.]

41 *Marksburg Castle* 6⅛ x 9⅜

Color etching. Atop a conical mtn. a castle high r. of ctr., tall keep rising in its ctr. Small town of Braubach at water's edge reflected ctr. and l. in wide bend of river, which, in this limited view, resembles a calm lake. Monogram r. [Locale: on r. bank of Rhine just above Coblenz. My copy: color; No. 46; Del. et Imp.; no title.]

42 *Piñon Trees and Spanish Peaks, Colorado* 6⅛ x 9⅜ (see Fig. 24)
Color etching. Two conical mtns., famous landmarks of southern Colorado, far distance r.; sunlit mesas middle distance r. In fgrd. l. a large rounded mass of piñon pines with dark leaves. Faint outline of taller tree l. suggesting an incomplete erasure on copper plate. Hand-drawn monogram l. Cf. #46 *Spanish Peaks, Colorado* [no. 1], in color. [Burr's note on Phoenix Art Museum copy: "First experiment with color in Denver." An edition of about fifty. My copy: color; no title.]

43 *Longs Peak, Estes Park, Colorado* [no. 2] 6⅛ x 9⅜
Color etching. Imposing Longs Peak dominates scene. Lesser peaks in middle distance r. to l. with V-shaped separation of peaks at far l. Trees on mtn. slopes fgrd. Diffused effect softens lines. Monogram r. Cf. #48 *Longs Peak from North Denver*. [Burr's note on Brooklyn Museum copy: "Done in oil color at one printing by George Elbert Burr."]

44 *Evening, North Wales* 6⅛ x 9⅜
Color etching. Pastoral scene with sheep on l. Stone cottages closely grouped ctr. Trees ctr. and l. Large trees r. of ctr., behind shepherdess, break sky-line made by verdure-clad mtn. slope descending sharply from upper r. Distant mtns. l. No monogram. [Burr's choice of colors produced striking variations in successive prints. My copy: color; No. 18; no title.]

45 *Oberwesel on Rhine, Night* 6⅛ x 9⅜
Color etching. Viewed from mountainside, Rhine curves from upper ctr. to lower l. corner. Three boats spiraling smoke. In far distance, Pfalz Castle built on rock midstream. Mtns. rise l. of river. On near side of river in ascending levels, houses and buildings of Oberwesel, church (Frauenkirche) with steeple, and, high on mtn., ruins of Schönburg Castle with flat-topped towers. Two light spots: moon in upper r. and its reflection on Rhine. A few trees in fgrd. No monogram.

46 *Spanish Peaks, Colorado* [no. 1] 6¾ x 9¾
Color etching. Large, twin conical peaks of the Culebra Range prominent in distance. In some prints they seem caught in first rays of sun; in others, in the alpenglow. In lower r. corner a clump of rounded trees partially obstructing view of distant mesas. Plains l. to r. with meandering stream bordered by several trees. Monogram usually on l.; some copies, no monogram. Cf. #42 *Piñon Trees and Spanish Peaks, Colorado*, nearly same size and also in color. See also #138 *Spanish Peaks* [no. 2], a color etching in larger size.

47 *Mt. Evans, Colorado* 6¾ x 9¾
Color etching. No aquatint. Large snow-covered ridge l. to r. forms skyline. Against a dark bgrd. of lesser peaks in middle distance, a low pyramidal peak can be distinguished jutting up r. of ctr. fgrd. Mtn. slope l. from above ctr. to midpoint, from which mtn. stream plunges straight to ctr. of bottom margin. Trees on slope l. Low vegetation and twisted tree lower r. Monogram r. [Possibly sketched along auto road to summit.]

48 *Longs Peak from North Denver* 7 x 10
Color etching. Sweeping view of snow-covered Longs Peak interrupted by lower mtn. Glimpse of snowy peak at far l. Large, level park in front of gently rolling foothills. A few houses and trees ctr. to r. middle distance. Stream mirroring

snowy peak r. fgrd. Scattered trees. Plants with pointed leaves on mtn. slope fgrd. Monogram l. Cf. #43 *Longs Peak, Estes Park, Colorado* [no. 2].

49   *Clear Creek from North Denver*   7 x 10
Color etching. Level, fertile valley floor. On r. a meandering stream with bridge; rounded trees, flat-topped mtns. l. to r., angular peaks above. The Range with snowy patches towering over all. Lower r. corner on plate: "DENVER COLO 1912." Monogram l.

50   *Village of Gandria, Lake Lugano, Italy*   5 x 8
Color etching. Mediterranean-type houses, four or more stories high, with red tile roofs and interesting shadows, from l. to r. of ctr., built on steep slope down to edge of lake and reflected in it. In ctr. of village a square tower with two high windows and surmounted by cross — the latter missing in some states. Trees above roofs and among houses. Water in fgrd. Two small boats near water's edge. Sketchy mtn. on r. Monogram l. [My copy: color; No. 15; Del. et Imp.; no title.]

51   *Rome from Pincio Garden*   7 x 10
Color etching. In ctr. fgrd. a fountain in circular pool enclosed by low, rounded rim; water plants, draped female figure (Pharaoh's daughter discovering the baby Moses hidden among the rushes). Sanded pathway. Stone bench r. and two standing figures. St. Peter's dome glimpsed through an opening in arched bower of trees. Monogram l. [This scene today is somewhat altered owing to growth of trees. My copy: color; No. 12; Del. et Imp.; no title.]

52   *Heidelberg, Sunset*[3]   6⅛ x 9⅜
Color etching. Uncommon view looking down Neckar River directly into sunset. Water flowing under eighteenth-century arched bridge of red stone. Grassy bank r. fgrd. Trees on bank near end of bridge. On opposite bank, in sunshine, lies venerable city of Heidelberg; from l. of ctr. to r., houses, steeple, etc., accented by sunlight. Mtn. slope close behind forms bgrd. at l. Many reflections in river. Monogram r.

53   *Coast of North Wales*   6⅛ x 9⅜
Color etching. A jutting, fissured escarpment in sunshine above narrow inlet. Higher rock wall on l. A ship, trailing smoke, high r. of ctr. where water and sky blend with no distinguishable horizon — a phenomenon effectively rendered in pale colors. Monogram r. [My copy: black and white; Trial Proof No. 1; on lower l. margin in Burr's handwriting, title, and "Six proofs only in this state."]

54   *Florence from San Miniato* [no. 1]   7 x 10
Color etching; some also pulled in black and white. Looking down, from plaza of Church of San Miniato al Monte, on Florence and the river Arno with three bridges — one of the outstanding panoramas in all Europe. Rain clouds far l. with puffy clouds in l. distance just above the surrounding hills. Clouds casting indefinite shadows on city. In middle distance far r., the tower of Palazzo Vecchio. Tall, straight cypress trees in r. fgrd. Other trees ctr. and l. suggest beginning

---

[3] As an aid in identifying untitled etchings in which a bridge figures more or less prominently, see #88 *Old Bridge, Chester* [no. 1]; #103 *Old Bridge, Coblenz*; #106 *Old Bridge, Isolabona, Italy*; #129 *Henkersteg, Nürnberg*; #144 *The Rhine at Laufenburg*; #240 *Ventimiglia, Italy*; #353 *Old Bridge, Chester, England* [no. 2]; #355 *Devil's Bridge near Lucca, Italy*. Several bridges appear in #54 *Florence from San Miniato* [no. 1]; #67 *Florence from San Miniato* [no. 2]; #345 *Sketch of Florence from San Miniato* [no. 3].

of Boboli Gardens. Etching extends to lower margin and fills corners l. and r. No monogram. Easily confused with #67 *Florence from San Miniato* [no. 2] (q.v.), which was made only in black and white. See also #345 *Sketch of Florence from San Miniato* [no. 3]. [My copy: brownish black ink on pale cream paper.]

55 *Street in Sierre, Suisse* 4¾ x 2¾; 3¾ x 2⅜

Mistakenly entitled *Street in Sion, Switzerland,* in American Etchers series, Vol. VII, and in *The Print Connoisseur* "Catalogue Raisonné." (Sion is another town on the Rhône, ten miles distant.) Street scene: houses with variety of roofs and small towers; an archway; an oriel (that can still be seen). Larger size: monogram l. Smaller size: street scene is in reverse; a woman with basket on back is added, as are capital letters spelling out "Sierre, Suisse" vertically, and "A Happy New Year to You" horizontally. Monogram l. [I surmise that the sole copy in this format that I have seen (NYPL) is possibly a unique offset print made for a special occasion, or person, after the original plate was cut and altered as described — although Burr may, of course, have made two separate plates.]

56 *Italian Village near Mentone* 4½ x 5½*

Have not found this etching. [The French town of Menton on the Riviera is near the present frontier. Road signs in both countries carry French and Italian spellings of the name.]

57 *An Archway, Bordighera* 4¾ x 3

Archway connects solid dark wall r. with house l. having outside stairway, doors, and window. Archway frames seascape with sailboats and tile-roofed building l. In ctr. of archway, sunk in wall, is small shrine to Virgin, its protecting doors standing open. Above are a column, flowers, pedestrian loitering on passageway afforded by archway. Monogram l. [See #243 *Bordighera, Italy* for further description of town.]

58 *Brown Palace Hotel, Denver* 6⅛ x 9⅜*

Have not found this etching. [Copyrighted before 1919. This venerable hostelry, faced with Arizona sandstone and Colorado red granite, is ten stories high, triangular in shape, with windows set into its rounded corners at each floor.]

59 *Old Cedar and Pikes Peak* 11½ x 9½

Base of graceful cedar tree r., a broken tree behind it at r. Exposed roots fastened to rocks, tree leaning l. to ctr., then straightening up and spreading branches and leaves. Snow-covered Pikes Peak towers over dark peaks whose descending slopes fold into each other. Clouds sketchily drawn. Rain streaks l. Some prints have cross lines as from a woven cloth pressed into the ground before plate is put into the acid bath but buffed out of white mtn.; others have this diffused effect only in r. upper corner; some trial proofs have none at all. Monogram r. Not to be confused with #226 *Pikes Peak, Colorado* (q.v.), in which trees are less prominent. [This view of Pikes Peak, near Colorado Springs, probably from north somewhere in Rampart Range. My copy: Del. et Imp.; no title.]

60 *Old Houses near Monte Carlo* 3½ x 3½

Composition forms right-angle triangle. Details finished from upper l. to lower r.; lower l. only suggested. Attention focused on upper stories of group of old houses.

George Elbert Burr

Capri from Sorrento Italy

FIGURE 38 — #245 *Capri from Sorrento* 10 x 7 inches

House on l. has two high archways under flat roof, high and open windows. On lower r. an arched entrance, low door, and steps leading down. A few birds in sky l. Sky crosshatched. Monogram l.

61 *First Snow* [no. 1]   3½ x 3½

Small snow scene. Group of trees ctr., branches tangled. Dark, icy stream fgrd. ctr. to low l. corner, vertical reflections in stream. White spots indicating snow on all tree branches. Snow-covered bushes in distance. Dark sky. Many small black dots throughout. Monogram r. Trees are similar to #270 *First Snow* [no. 2] (q.v.).

62 *Winter* [no. 1]   7 x 10

Wintry landscape. Group of large, leafless trees r. of ctr. with fallen, dead trees horizontal l. and r. Other scattered, snowy, deciduous trees beyond. Leaden sky, wet snow, small spots around black stream flowing r. to corner. Ground slightly concave. Monogram r. Not to be confused with #326 *Winter No. 2* (q.v.). [Said to have been sketched on his brother Linn's farm near Cameron, Mo.]

63 *Pity's at the Pool* [nude]   10 x 12

Beside a secluded and shady pool a dainty sylph, her hands raising strands of hair, standing in front of large, dark tree with thick, burled trunk, many twisted branches. Figure in half-light, only lower part reflected in water. Some water plants. Dense thicket forms low bgrd. Rather dark except for light sky that silhouettes branches and foliage. Mysterious. Monogram r. Cf. #145 *The Nightingale*. [Burr's title is clearly written, but the sense is obscure. Could he, perchance, have meant *Pixy's at the Pool?*]

64 *On the Little Colorado River, Arizona*   5 x 7

Desert landscape. Some dark trees on riverbank r. fgrd., figure on horseback in shade. Absence of clouds and frugality of line suggest arid brightness. Buttes and mesas in bgrd. entire l. to r. Monogram r. Cf. #70 *Near Chavez, New Mexico*. [The Little Colorado joins the Colorado near the eastern end of Grand Canyon National Park.]

65 *Near Ash Fork, Arizona*   5 x 7

Landscape with mtn. range in far distance forming entire bgrd., highest in ctr. R. half of middle distance, a mesa. Gently rolling slopes with rounded trees in fgrd. Sky filled with fine horizontal lines. Some white clouds. Monogram l.

66 *A New England Road* [no. 1]   7 x 10

A landscape with trees, house, stone and split-rail fences, man at well sweep l. of ctr. Roadway r. of ctr. On r., two trees, wagon frame against shed. Rolling mtns. in bgrd. Luminous and drifting clouds. Monogram l. Cf. #267 *A New England Road* [no. 2], the same, trimmed and reworked.

67 *Florence from San Miniato* [no. 2]   7 x 10

Looking down on Florence and the river Arno. Three bridges, the Ponte Vecchio in middle. Buildings on l. and r. of river. Dark trees form lower frame, gracefully fading to corners l. and r. Cloud shadows on surrounding hills, one dark cloud shadow on Florence behind tower of Palazzo Vecchio. Monogram l. Easily confused with #54 *Florence from San Miniato* [no. 1] (q.v.) in color and also in black and white. See also #345 *Sketch of Florence from San Miniato* [no. 3].

George Elbert Burr   Trial proof.

Figure 39 — #248 *From Appian Way, Rome*   6 x 9 inches

68   *Arizona Clouds* [no. 1]   7 x 10
Color mezzotint. Thick, beautiful clouds above cloud streaks drifting over vast expanse of flat desert with distant mesas ctr. l. to r. Spotty desert vegetation in fgrd., an arroyo l. of ctr. Rain streaks far r. Monogram r. Printed in black and white after slight reworking of plate, this becomes #184 *Arizona Clouds* [no. 2] (q.v.), the first in the Desert Set. This was Burr's only mezzotint plate; he is quoted by Leila Mechlin in *The American Magazine of Art*, XX (1929), 333, as saying, "I only resorted to mezzotint once, just to see if I could do it. I did it, but never again. It's a slow, plodding process, not adapted to my temperament." (See *Mezzotint* in Glossary.) [My copy: color; Del. et Imp.; no title.]

69   *St. Saphorin, Lake Geneva*   6⅛ x 9⅜; 5½ x 7⅞
Small figure of man walking on street in St. Saphorin (above Vevay), rake on shoulder, spotlighted by sun. Houses high l., high bank r., tall, straight tree, houses and church tower, ctr. Angles softened by trees. Bright spot in sky. All details fade to edges. Monogram r. [My copy (larger size): not marked "trial proof"; a presentation copy on thin paper dated June 4, 1913.]

70   *Near Chavez, New Mexico*   5 x 8
Desert landscape. Flat-topped butte r., mtns. l. Man on horseback l. of ctr. Spots of sagebrush add interest. Sparsity of lines. Monogram r. Cf. #64 *On the Little Colorado River, Arizona.* [The spelling "Chaves" is found in early catalogues.]

71   *Pikes Peak from Manitou*   7 x 10
Color etching. Mtn. landscape from near summit of Mt. Manitou. Pikes Peak fills bgrd. Mtns. in middle distance slope down from either side and converge in ctr. Trees and rocks in lower r. corner. Monogram l. [My copy: color; Del. et Imp.; No. 13; no title. Duplicate copy: black and white; "Trial proof unfinished"; no title.]

72   *The Fairy Glen, Bettws-y-coed, North Wales*   8 x 5
A dark, quiet pool ctr. in narrow, steep, rocky glen. Nearly vertical upended rocks l. Opening in narrow gulley ctr., trees above, allowing light to filter down. Vertical rock wall middle distance r. Interesting contrasts of light and shade. Monogram r. [My copy: in Burr's handwriting, ". . . shown (1915) at the Panama-Pacific Exposition at San Francisco." Wales, like Ireland, has a rich heritage of fairy lore. The town (also spelled Betws-y-coed) is on the Llugwy near its confluence with the Conway. The Fairy Glen is on the latter. Another river, the Lledr, joins the Conway close by. Beautiful views of three river valleys, hills, and the mtn. Moel Siabod, all sketched by Burr circa 1900.]

73   *The Willows*   7¾ x 5   (see Fig. 31)
Standing l. of placid pool, a group of half-dead willows, holes in trunks, some dead branches; other trees r. on farther shore, their light trunks mirrored in quiet pond with lily pads and other water plants. Heavy shade in fgrd. Monogram l. [My copy: title on lower l. edge of lower margin.]

74   *Mt. Byers, Colorado*   7 x 10
Color etching. Skyline composed of one sharp, snow-covered peak in ctr. with other snowy mountaintops far l. and r. In middle distance and l. of summit of Mt. Byers, a smaller, dark, sharp-pointed mtn., the peak cutting skyline. Dark mtn. ridges slope gently from both l. and r. edges, meeting in ctr. Twisting stream

r. fgrd. reflects light. Clumps of trees in lower corners. Monogram l. [Mt. Byers is west of Denver in the conglomerate beyond the Front Range. My copy: color; No. 9; Del. et Imp.; no title. Duplicate copy: color; all margins cropped.]

75   *Venetian Fishing Boats*   12 x 10
Color etching. Most of print area filled with boats, sails, fishing nets hanging to dry, and dark reflections. Of secondary importance are white church and small sailboats l., and their reflections in water. Other boats r. Monogram r. Cf. #246 *Venice after Storm.*

76   *Street in San Remo*   10 x 7   (see Fig. 32)
Street scene, five archways built between buildings, one showing above another. Partial archway l. and house wall with outside stairway, windows in wall, one framing bust of woman looking out. Woman at top of stairway holding child. Five figures in street, one with tall cane, one a child. Chimney pots above roofs. Strong contrast of light and dark. Monogram r. [Awarded second prize for etchings at Colorado State Fair at Pueblo; his #137 *Winter Morning* took first prize (*Rocky Mountain News*, Sept. 28, 1919, sect. "Art News"). San Remo is on the Italian Riviera, high above the Mediterranean. The oldest section, portrayed here, was damaged in World War II.]

77   *Red Roofs of Siena*   7 x 10
Color etching. Some printed in black and white. Mass of rooftops pitched at similar angles. In ctr. a two-storied house has arched arcade at ground level, windows above. Soft screening of trees at lower border. Sketchily suggested on horizon are Cathedral r., a campanile ctr., another church dome far l. "SIENA" on plate r. corner. Monogram l. [My copy: black and white. Color is more effective: it accentuates the red tile roofs so common throughout Italy.]

78   *Stunted Cedars*   7 x 10;* 5 x 8*
Have not found this etching.

79   *Charcoal Boat, Venice* [no. 1]   5 x 8*
Have not found this etching. [See #279 *Old Charcoal Boat, Venice* (no. 3), an etching, and #352 *Charcoal Boat, Venice* (no. 2), a drypoint. All are identical in size.]

80   *Windsor Castle, Evening*   7 x 10
Castle on far side of Thames, trees along bank. The crenelated Round Tower prominent in ctr. General impression of many buildings filling skyline l. of ctr. to r. Roofs of all descriptions — Gothic, peaked, flat. Clouds l. emphasize contour of black tree l. Vegetation in r. corner on near side of river. © & "GEO. E. BURR" on plate r. corner. Monogram l. Cf. #84 *Warwick Castle, Night.*

81   *Oaks in Winter* [no. 1]   10 x 7
Cold and damp-looking winter scene. One large oak r. of ctr. growing beside stake-and-rider fence. Other trees l. and r., all snow-spotted. Snow came from r. Ground slopes gently down to l. Trees in distance nearly white. Some copies have monogram l., others no monogram. Cf. #271 *Oaks in Winter* [no. 2], a reworked version.

82 *High Street, Oxford* 10 x 12 (see Fig. 33)
View from ctr. of High Street as rain is slackening. On l. University College, on r. other colleges; sharp-pointed steeples of University Church and All Saints Church. Pedestrians, horse-drawn carts. Sunshine on some buildings, not on others. Atmospheric conditions superbly portrayed. Monogram l. [My copy: title hand-printed on face of window mat.]

83 *Evening, Lake Geneva* 12 x 10
Color etching. Thirteenth-century Castle of Chillon on water's edge l., trees close against it. Snow-capped peaks of the Dents du Midi, and dark mtn. (Grammont, on south side of the lake near French border) rising before them to r. Sailing craft with two lateen sails, turned broadside r. to ctr., and reflections, occupy about two-thirds of total area. Bright clouds r., but streaks l. suggest rain. Monogram l. [Copies I have seen were predominantly in shades of blue, appropriate to the celebrated color of Lake Geneva.]

84 *Warwick Castle, Night* 7 x 10
Dark black-and-white print (American Etchers series, Vol. VII, lists as a color etching, a form with which I am unfamiliar). Chiaroscuro effect, tower in bright moonlight l. of ctr. Castle walls in semidarkness. Lacy pattern of trees, black against dark grays of castle and sky. Dark reflections in river Avon. Monogram r. Cf. #80 *Windsor Castle, Evening.*

85 *Elms, Windsor* 7 x 10
Color etching. Pastoral scene; grazing cows under large, spreading trees on r., all heading l. Shade, small pond, and grass. On l. similar trees more distant. Interesting contrasts of light and shade. Monogram r.

86 *Temple of the Sibyl, Tivoli* 10 x 7
Small, circular Roman temple with columns, standing majestically and alone on farther edge of gorge, a guardrail and posts in front of it, a mass of soft-looking bushes or treetops covering slopes below it. Contrast of pale classical delicacy with irregularity of dark trees framing temple on three sides. In trial proof first state, monogram r.; in published edition, monogram l., but can be discovered r. also among lines denoting foliage.

87 *Low Tide, North Wales* [no. 1] 7 x 10
Dark print. Two beached sailboats, scarcely visible, masts leaning at different angles. Dark water, dark sky, bright clouds behind black, stormy clouds. Small sails on water in distance. Some water in fgrd. Monogram r. Cf. #357 *Low Tide, North Wales* [no. 2], probably made from same sketch.

88 *Old Bridge, Chester* [no. 1] 5 x 8
From l. the approach and four irregular arches of old stone bridge, light striking ctr. At r. a tall, seven-storied building with two arched channels ctr. at water level, a cluster of lower, odd-shaped buildings to r., one tall chimney—the famous Mills of Dee, which stood on r. bank until 1909. Water from r. corner flows under bridge ctr. Positions of several small boats in water and on shore suggest low tide. Fisherman standing on bank l. House l. and trees make bgrd. for bridge. Rocker marks at edges of etching. Monogram r. of ctr. Made from same sketch as #353 *Old Bridge, Chester, England* [no. 2], the latter in soft ground and drypoint. [Bridge over the river Dee, just before it widens and

FIGURE 40 — #264 *Fish Creek, Apache Trail, Arizona* 6⅝ x 4⅞ inches

Compare circled profile with that at bottom of remarque. *Courtesy of Prints Division, New York Public Library, Astor, Lenox & Tilden Foundations*

empties into the Irish Sea, has one end in England, the other in Wales. See #52 *Heidelberg, Sunset* and footnote listing other bridges.]

89   *Street in Old Lausanne*   5 x 8*

Have not found this etching. [This city, built on the slopes of Mont Jorat just above the port of Ouchy on Lake Geneva, has interesting old houses, streets on several levels, striking panoramic vistas.]

90   *Amalfi*   5 x 8

Steep, rocky shoreline l. built up with numerous houses; many windows. Other houses and trees on steep mountainside. Mtn. skyline ctr. and suggested to r. One small boat in water near shore, others on shore. A few figures. On r. an expanse of water. Sketchy. Monogram l. [Burr's note on NYPL copy: "Trial proof, first state, never finished." Amalfi, southeast of Naples on Gulf of Salerno, is approximately at midpoint of beautiful Amalfi Drive. This view is from site of former Convento dei Cappuccini, which became a hotel about the time Burr was there.]

91   *Pisa*   5 x 8

Horizontal line of interest. Long, straight wall and small trees l. of ctr. Small building and tall, straight trees to r. The Campanile (Leaning Tower) l. of ctr. beyond Cathedral and Baptistry. Two people on path r. of ctr. fgrd. in open field that suggests flatness of Arno valley. Apennines sketched in bgrd. Monogram l.

92   *Valley of the Lledr, North Wales* [no. 1]   5 x 8

Deep, rather wide valley ctr., low mtns. on either side. Rounded trees ctr., sketchy stone fences above banks l. Far distance light gray, middle distance shades of gray with shadows, fgrd. ctr. and r. in heavy drypoint. Small stone cottage ctr. partially hidden by trees. Fades to edges. Monogram r. For reworked version see # 316 *Valley of the Lledr, Wales* [no. 2].

93   *From My Cabin Window*   5 x 8

Dramatic soft ground. Stormy clouds in bright sky almost surrounded by dark sky, dark clouds, rain streaks, and dark treetops. Sunlit mesas form low horizon. In l. corner of fgrd. a sharply descending mtn. slope with a few trees. Monogram l. Similar, except for size, to #213 *Cloudburst*.

94   *Moel Siabod, North Wales*   5 x 8

Sun strikes high meadow rising from valley toward summit of Moel Siabod while rain is falling r. Large sheep graze in r. fgrd. Rounded trees between sheep and high meadow. River Llugwy lower l. Misty air. Monogram r. Cf. #354 *Valley of the Llugwy, Wales*.

95   *Barnegat Light*   5 x 8; 5 x 7⅛*   (see Fig. 12)

In fgrd. a small man seated on gunwale of rowboat, gazing out to sea r., legs crossed, smoking a pipe, fish pole drooping. Boat's painter cast on the sand l. Lighthouse in distance l. of ctr., several houses, boathouse, and trees. Two figures strolling along shore r. distance. In far distance r. dark, drifting smoke calls attention to two ships on horizon. Many birds in sky. Monogram l. [This suggests a casual self-portrait.]

96   *Sketches near Longmont, Colorado*   10 x 7

Three sketches on one plate, separated later. Top: white mtn. behind dark mtns. Monogram r. This becomes #118 *Longs Peak from Longmont, Colorado*. Middle: mtn. bgrd. with haystacks in fgrd. Monogram r. This becomes #155 *The Range from Longmont, Colorado.* Bottom: river, trees, reflections in water. Monogram l. This becomes #99 *North Boulder Creek, Colorado.*

97 *Autumn* [no. 1]   4⅜ x 2⅞*

Have not found this etching. [These measurements, given in American Etchers series, Vol. VII, and in *The Print Connoisseur* "Catalogue Raisonné," may possibly be transposed.]

98 *A Santa Barbara Road*   6 x 4⅜; 3¾ x 3⅜

Misshapen tree with forked trunk standing r. leaning l., casting its shadow on roadway beneath it. Trees in bgrd. l. and ctr. Mtn. low r. A few birds in sky r. Monogram r. of ctr. [My copies: larger size, Del. et Imp., no title; smaller size, no title. Larger size not labeled "trial proof"; Burr may have put a number into circulation before deciding to cut the plate and make slight changes. Used by Burr as Christmas card, 1913.]

99 *North Boulder Creek, Colorado*   3⅞ x 6⅞

Cut from bottom of #96 *Sketches near Longmont, Colorado.* Landscape at dusk. Large trees ctr. to r., dark and lacy against bright spot in sky and reflecting darkly in water in fgrd. Dark foothills receding into high mtns. of the Front Range, which are in more light and blend into sky. At extreme r. just in front of mtns. are park, trees, and house. Monogram l. [My copy: monogram indistinguishable.]

100 *Old Cottonwoods* [no. 1]   7 x 5

Trees with pale, divided trunks, some leaves, live and dead entangled branches. Dark trees in bgrd. Monogram r. Somewhat similar trees with divided trunks occur in #134 *Old Haw Trees.*

101 *Rhine at Caub*   4¾ x 7

Color etching. Looking downstream, a sweeping curve of river from lower l. to ctr. Small town (Caub) r. middle distance. Another town (Oberwesel) across river l. with ruins of Schönburg Castle on mountaintop above it. Mtns. form entire bgrd. Clouds, more prominent in some prints than in others. Monogram r. Smallest of the color etchings. [My copy: color; Del. et Imp.; no title.]

102 *The Desert* [no. 1]   7 x 10

Color etching. Desert scene; in middle distance a heavily laden wagon with cloth cover, two sizes of wheels, being pulled through sandy expanse by a pair of horses heading r. Sparse vegetation in fgrd. Mtns. in bgrd. Lovely cloud effects. "GEB 1914" on plate r. Monogram r. Cf. #262 *The Desert, Arizona* [no. 2], a black-and-white version slightly reworked.

103 *Old Bridge, Coblenz*   5 x 7¼

Three and one-half spans of medieval St. Balduin's Bridge over the Mosel (Moselle). On r. end a round tower with hexagonal roof and steeple. Wall at lower r., two figures near wall, two figures nearer river's edge, and stairs leading down. Other buildings beyond end of bridge. On bridge a horsecart, figures. Birds in sky. Two small boats seen through span near edge of river. Monogram r. [See #52 *Heidelberg, Sunset* and footnote listing other bridges.]

104   *The Rhine below St. Goar*   4⅞ x 7¾
Dramatic soft ground. Looking downstream, ruins of thirteenth-century Rheinfels Castle on steep mountainside l. A few trees in lower l. corner. River low ctr. Mtns. in distance. Clouds. Monogram l.

105   *Clear Creek Meadows, Denver* [no. 1]   4 x 7
Landscape of flat park, groups of rounded trees, female figure ctr. bgrd., house beyond, and cabin ctr. far r. Bgrd. formed by flat-topped mtns. with Front Range just beyond, Longs Peak rising pale and high in distance far r. Bright-edged clouds low, dark sky above. Etching low on sheet. No superfluous lines. Monogram l. Copyright circa 1914. Cf. #143 *The Range from Denver*. [My copy: Del. et Imp.; no title.]

106   *Old Bridge, Isolabona, Italy*   5 x 3¾; 4⅞ x 3⅜
Near a high, one-arched stone bridge with plants and vines growing out of it, a woman ctr. fgrd. beside stream, bending over a washing. Child stands near-by. On l. old houses, two arches, many windows. A figure l. resting on bridge. In ctr. bgrd. a mtn. rising from near stream bed. Monogram r. on larger size, l. on smaller size. [For locale see #7 *Isolabona, Italy*. My copy: no title. See #52 *Heidelberg, Sunset* and footnote listing other bridges.]

107   *Windswept, Estes Park*   3½ x 3⅜
Two trees l. with gnarled trunks, some leaves, windblown branches to r. almost resembling humans with long hair streaming in wind. Roots partly exposed. To r., Mt. Meeker and Longs Peak, snow on slopes and caught in ravines. Gray sky, gray ground. Light through ctr., dark tops of lower mtns. in middle distance r. Monogram l. below tree roots. This is either #16 *Study of Pines* [no. 2] before plate was cut and reworked, or a separate plate with many of the same details. [Used by Burr as Christmas card, 1915.]

108   *Our Cabin*   5¼ x 4   (see Fig. 14)
Large boulders and rocks directly above small cabin with porch across front. Section of tilting rock strata in fgrd. Scattered small trees; one in front of cabin resembles Christmas tree. Monogram l. [Made directly on plate as Burr saw it, hence scene is reversed. My copy: dark gray paper; Del. et Imp.; on mount, "With the seasons greeting. George E. Burr. Dec. 1914"; title on lower edge of mount not in Burr's handwriting.]

109   *Patience*   3 x 5
Donkey with saddle blanket, hitched to ring in wall below crossed bars protecting window l. Four doorways in angle of small paved court. Strong, bright light and absence of people suggest siesta time in Italy. Monogram r.

110   *Windswept Pine* [no. 2]   5 x 3
Growing out of solid rock, a twisted pine shaped like reversed number seven; leaves on horizontal branches. Cracked and fissured rock, barren except for tree. Edge of rock slants from lower l. to above ctr. at r. Clouds above. Glimpse of park low l. Two birds in sky. Monogram r. Cf. #142 *Chimney Rock;* also #115 *The Twisted Pine*, the same size.

111   *Old Houses, Sierre*   3½ x 3; 3 x 2½*
Ctr. to r. a large house, windows and shutters, three arches, square tower at l. end with sharp, pointed roof. Shadows below overhanging roofs. Fades to r.

© George Elbert Burr

Cloud Shadows Apache Trail Ariz

FIGURE 41 — #268 *Cloud Shadows, Apache Trail, Arizona* 8 x 10 inches

edge. L. of ctr. a wagon with two sizes of wheels, a barn, mtns. in bgrd. Monogram l. [My copy: sepia; no title. Used by Burr as Christmas card, 1914.]

112 *Moonlight* 5 x 3

Three tall, straight trees growing out of rocks l. of ctr. occupying fgrd. Faint mesa in distance r. Full moon lower third r. Many horizontal lines all through sky and valley. Monogram r.

113 *Washing Place, Villeneuve* 3 x 4

In town square, a woman doing her laundry at public fountain; she is leaning over her work, skirts fastened up protectively. Two tubs on wide wall, water spouting from pipes just above. Bgrd. formed by house wall with windows, shutters, doorway. Shadows cast to r. Monogram r. [Just such a place can be found today in this town at head of Lake Geneva.]

114 *Geoffrey's Window, Monmouth* 5 x 3

Plain-looking old walls made of square stones, with two-tiered bay window, stone tracery beginning at level of second story. Five windows can be seen in both tiers, some standing open. Two closed doors below. Young boy l. fgrd. Monogram r. [Title refers to chronicler of Arthurian legend, Geoffrey of Monmouth (d. 1154).]

115 *The Twisted Pine* 5 x 3

A contorted limber pine growing out of rocks near timber line, its dark trunk ctr. forming imperfect letter S, a clump of greenery at its base. Deep-set valley l. Sun and sunburst with streaks of rays from slightly r. of ctr. Low, dark clouds. Monogram l. Cf. #110 *Windswept Pine* [no. 2], the same size; also #142 *Chimney Rock*. [My copy: printed on folded sheet; no title; facing on other half of folder, in pencil, "With the Seasons greetings from Cousin 'Bert,' Dec. 1921."]

116 *On Lake Como* 3 x 4

House r. built on rocks at water level, small arching bridge connecting with another building, extreme r., both in Mediterranean style. Beyond are trees and houses on sharply rising bank l. of ctr. ascending toward r. Rolling clouds. Lower third is water. Monogram r.

117 *The Rhine at Rheinstein* 4 x 5

View south from west bank of Rhine. Castle on steep rocky cliff, tree growing next to it and near cliff's edge. Mtn. slope on r. terraced with vineyards, descending toward river. Curving shore line r. Full moon upper r. Moonlight strikes water, making light horizontal streak. Light and dark streaks in sky accenting dark boat midstream, pale smoke rising from it. Misty effect. No monogram.

118 *Longs Peak from Longmont, Colorado* 4 x 7

Cut from #96 *Sketches near Longmont, Colorado*, at top of plate. Longs Peak, snow-clad and majestic, stands above dark mtns. in middle distance. Flat valley with trees and fence rows. Small house r. of ctr. Monogram r.

119 *Château at Aigle* 3 x 5

Castle with towers and sharp-pointed spires ctr. to r. on a rise of ground and set off by a few trees. Beyond, in broad Rhône valley near head of Lake Geneva, is town of Aigle. Dark mtn., etched with many fine lines, rising from far bank of river. High skyline, the pinnacled approaches to the Dents du Midi. Narrow strip of sky filled in with horizontal lines. Monogram r. [This Gothic structure now houses inmates of the Prisons du District. Used by Burr as Christmas card. My copy: no title.]

120 *Santa Barbara Live Oaks* 3¼ x 4¾

Two enormous, spreading, rounded trees, the focus of attention in small, charming landscape on seacoast. A few rocks in meadow l. Hills and mtns. r. Stream winding on r. Two tiny figures under trees. Horizon ctr. is water. Monogram r. [Used by Burr as Christmas card. My two copies: no title.]

121 *Thames at Windsor* 3¾ x 4¾

Dividing line of interest straight l. to r. Trees above bank, reflections below. Near shore l. two figures, woman wearing large hat, man standing at rear of boat, sculling. Rooftops, ctr. r., half hidden among trees. A few birds in sky l. Areas of reflections and areas of no reflections lend important interest. Monogram r.

122 *Twilight* [no. 1] 2¾ x 3⅞

Peaceful, intimate Colorado landscape. Large cumulus cloud r. of ctr. caught in afterglow in vast expanse of dark sky. Mesas and mtns. form distant bgrd. beyond rolling plains. Gentle mtn. slope with two prominent trees l. Steeper mtn. slope r. Fgrd. r. has rocks in sunlight, a few dark trees. Monogram l.

123 *Old Cedar, Manitou* 5½ x 7

One lone, twisted, gnarled tree in great detail, growing out of rocks r., contrasting with white-clad Pikes Peak l. in distance. Monogram r.

124 *Evening* 12 x 10

A slender dead tree standing alone l. of ctr. in swampy water showing ripples and reflections. Dark evergreens form bgrd. Clouds r. of ctr. low in sky. Dark vegetation l. and r. lower corners. © & "GEO. E. BURR" on plate lower r. Monogram l. [In some copies a delicate crisscross of lines in pale areas.]

125 *Catania Gate, Taormina, Sicily* 10 x 7 (see Fig. 34)

An ancient stone gate, part of city wall formerly surrounding Taormina. In ctr. fgrd. on rough roadway, a woman balancing a slender, two-handled earthen jug on her head, at her side a small girl. Behind them a portal with pointed arch leading into opaque passageway. At a sharp angle l. the gate abuts a taller stone building with high archway l. and three windows. At juncture, a narrow, outside stone stairway with no handrail ascends to roof line. In r. fgrd. a low wall. Above it and in far distance, a small landscape of hills and valleys and the snow-covered cone of Mt. Etna. Monogram & © l. [This gate, near the Piazza Sant' Antonio, was destroyed in 1943 during World War II. My copy: *Catania Gate* lower l. on bottom margin, not in Burr's handwriting.]

126 *Old Fountain, Taormina, Sicily* 9¾ x 7½

Ancient, tall fountain in the Piazza del Duomo mounted on three nearly circular stone steps forming base. Surmounting two spilling basins, each supported by small carved stone figures, is statue of the Minotaur, the emblem of Taormina. Two small columns topped by carved stone animals (horses with serpent tails, bodies couchant), one in ctr. spouting water beside water jug. Another jug on pavement below fountain. Two women l. of ctr., one seated on step, one standing. In bgrd. a house with window and solid door; both have rounded, arched tops. A smaller building very close to it on r. has rectangular window, decorations above lintel. Low wall r., post and vines. Monogram & © l.

127 *Neuthor, Nürnberg*   7 x 5½; 3½ x 7*
Built into ancient wall surrounding historic Old Town, a medieval round tower with dark, squat shingled roof and cupola, all exquisitely fine-lined. In front nestles a stone house, its shingled roof at various levels shown in great detail. Two archways into house, woman and child at nearer archway. Around the house, trees whose delicate tracery adds a softening, decorative effect. Rounded clouds. Interesting, strong contrasts of dark and light. Monogram & © l. [The dimensions 3½ x 7 given in American Etchers series, Vol. VII, and in *The Print Connoisseur* "Catalogue Raisonné," are clearly wrong.]

128 *Walpurgiskapelle, Nürnberg*   7 x 5½
In ctr. a small stone church built on a hill, bell mounted at peak of sharply pitched roof, slender poplar rising beyond. Tall building with chimney abuts on r. Half-timbered two-storied house l. Two figures under small tree ctr. At r. a picket fence, small trees and shrubs. Path and steps leading down ctr. Sketchy clouds. Monogram & © l. [This chapel, built on site of earlier ones that had stood in Old Town beside the castle, was erected in 1492 and later rebuilt. It was named for St. Walpurgis, Abbess of Heidenheim (d. 778), whose Saint's Day is May 1. Legendary Walpurgisnacht is the night of April 30—May 1. Almost totally destroyed in 1945 during war.]

129 *Henkersteg, Nürnberg*   5½ x 7
Ctr. and l. the stone two-span, covered Hangman's Bridge (fourteenth century) over the Pegnitz in Old Town. On l. end of bridge two small towers. Trees l. fgrd. At r. end just r. of ctr. the tall, square Water Tower, two rows of windows near top. Farther r. a half-timbered house with sharply slanting roof, tall chimney, many windows, overhanging balconies on two stories. Water l. of ctr. to lower r. edge of paper. Burr did not reverse his sketch: the scene appears as in a mirror. Monogram & © l. [The large building is the Weinstadel, so named from its use in the sixteenth century as a wine storage. It is now a home for university students. See #52 *Heidelberg, Sunset* and footnote listing other bridges.]

130 *Insel Schütt, Nürnberg*   5½ x 7
View of tranquil water as it flows around Schütt Island in Pegnitz River, in Old Town. Houses built to water's edge l., large and small domes rising above them in ctr. Black roofs. Man in small boat. Footbridge and tree r. Reflections. Monogram & © l. [My copy: *In Nurnburg* (sic); trial proof.]

131 *Windswept Spruces*   7 x 5½
Triangular group of sharp-pointed spruces near timber line r., all limbs forced to grow to l. Fallen trees at l., rocks in fgrd. Sharp peaks l., white peaks beyond. Clouds close to mountaintop. Monogram & © l. Similar to #20 *Study of Pines* [no. 6] (q.v.), but larger.

132 *Home of the Winds* [no. 1]   5½ x 7
Ragged, storm-tossed trees near timber line leaning far to r., some fallen. Dark mtn. far distance r. with sharp points, snow in ravines. Stormy sky, scudding

© George Elbert Burr

© George Elbert Burr

FIGURE 42 — #274 *Evening, Apache Trail, Arizona*   5 x 7 inches

clouds, rain or sleet blowing from upper l. downward to r. Monogram & © l. Not to be confused with #133 *Timberline Pine* (q.v.). Cf. #139 *Home of the Winds* [no. 2], similar and larger. [My copy: title lower l. edge of bottom margin.]

133 *Timberline Pine* 5½ x 7

Gnarled, windswept tree ctr. Fallen trees with jagged branches and some rocks in fgrd. Distant mtns. r. of ctr., snow on summits and in ravines; one r. of ctr. is star-shaped. Ominous sky with light spot behind tree. Many dark lines in sky. Strong contrast of black and white. Monogram & © l. Not to be confused with #132 *Home of the Winds* [no. 1] (q.v.). [Ypsilon Mountain in Rocky Mountain National Park has fissures which, when snow-filled at some times of the year, have this pattern. My copy: black ink on white paper; no title. Duplicate copy: brown ink on cream-color paper; no title; Del. et Imp.; less turbulence in sky.]

134 *Old Haw Trees* 7 x 10

Clumps of trees with divided trunks, ctr. Rocks rise slightly on either side. Light coming from l. shines on trunks and ground near them. Light sky behind trees. Fairly level horizon of dark mesas. Dark leaves, dark shade, light trunks. "GEO. E. BURR" on some prints l. on plate, not on others. Monogram r. For somewhat similar trees with divided trunks see #100 *Old Cottonwoods* [no. 1].

135 *Sentinel Pine* 10 x 7

One large, strong old pine, trunk slightly curving, standing on mountainside among rocks, overlooking plains and mesas. Shadows cast near base of tree. Subtle cloud effects just above horizon. Monogram l. [Burr wrote an accompanying poem that appeared in the *Denver Times*, Mar. 30, 1916, p. 3, containing these lines:

> An aged pine, alone on wind-swept hill stands sentinel
> Over rolling plain and rocky rampart of the Snowy Range.

The Culebra Range (local name, Snowy Range) includes the Spanish Peaks. My copy: Del. et Imp.; no title.]

136 *Winter Evening* 10 x 7

In ctr. a tangled mass of leafless trees and shrubs with intertwined branches, all spotted with wet, clinging snow. Icy stream from ctr. to lower r. Gray and lowering sky. Path of diffused light gleams across lower third. Skyline just above ctr. from l. to r., dipping slightly behind trees. Monogram l.

137 *Winter Morning* 10 x 12

Damp-looking winter scene. Bare, snow-spotted trees and tangles of bushes along bank of black stream that curves from ctr. r., spreading out to lower l. Intricate patterns of branches. Dark sky. Monogram r. [Awarded Silver Medal from St. Paul (Minnesota) Institute, 1916. The medal, designed by Paul Manship, is reproduced in *Rocky Mountain News*, Apr. 23, 1916, and in *The American Magazine of Art*, VII (Apr. 1916). In 1919 *Winter Morning* was awarded a first prize at Colorado State Fair, as noted under #76 *Street in San Remo*.]

138 *Spanish Peaks* [no. 2] 10 x 12

Color etching. Two large, pointed peaks rise in bgrd. high above mesas in middle distance. In fgrd., water reflects group of trees l. of ctr. and smaller group r. Broad expanse of arid grazing land between fgrd. and bgrd. Depending on the colors Burr used, these two peaks are in sunlight or caught in the alpenglow. Monogram r. Cf. #227 *Old Cedars and Spanish Peaks, Colorado*. See also #46 *Spanish Peaks, Colorado* [no. 1], in color.

139 *Home of the Winds* [no. 2] 10 x 12

Color etching. Some in black and white. Group of tangled, storm-tossed trees leaning from r. to l. From extreme r. a large, misshapen limber pine with split trunk leaning over spruces and other trees, whose branches are on only one side of trunks. Mass of low-growing verdure r. fgrd. Deep valleys l. Dramatic effect of storm clouds; streaks of rain or sleet only in sky. Monogram & © r. This is larger version of #132 *Home of the Winds* [no. 1] (q.v.) and reversed; trees lean in opposite direction. Cf. also #228 *Timberline Storm*.

140 *Old Cottonwoods* [no. 2] 10 x 12 (see Fig. 35)

Light on rolling clouds behind two large, spreading trees silhouettes individual leaves and backlights them. Exquisite detail both dark and light. Trees form dark inverted triangle superimposed on white cloud mass surrounded by dark sky. Shallow-appearing water with reflections ctr. fgrd. Middle-distance interest in streak of light, house r., haystack l. of ctr., and a few trees. Monogram & © l.

141 *Marblehead, Fisherman's Home* 3 x 5

Precarious position and angularity of small house with beams and frame support, and cluster of accompanying shacks all perched on rocks, contrast with placid water. Small boat, lighthouse, distant rocks l. of ctr. Overturned rowboat and lobster pots on rocky bank r. Monogram r.

142 *Chimney Rock* 3½ x 2

Eroded rock standing vertically ctr. One tree growing out of rock l., a few other trees low l. Boulder r. fgrd. Monogram upper l. Cf. #110 *Windswept Pine* [no. 2] and #115 *The Twisted Pine,* both larger.

143 *The Range from Denver* 3 x 5

Broad park l. to r., small stream r., with verdure along banks. Many trees r., both round and pointed; clumps of trees in middle distance. On l. dark mtns. in front of range of white mtns. Birds in sky. Monogram l. Similar to #105 *Clear Creek Meadows, Denver* [no. 1] (q.v.) and smaller.

144 *The Rhine at Laufenburg* 3¾ x 5

Ancient, picturesque bridge connecting Germany and Switzerland, where Rhine flows westerly toward Basel. Bridge, from l. to r.: slender span, open handrail, two pedestrians; covered ctr. span; solid stone approach from river bank. Cluster of buildings; higher on r., church with steeple. Narrow, rocky river bed bends from ctr. to l. fgrd. Monogram r. [Burr did not reverse his sketch. This bridge was later replaced (1911); blasting, and a hydroelectric plant downstream, have slightly altered the appearance of the channel and its banks. See #52 *Heidelberg, Sunset* and footnote listing other bridges.]

145 *The Nightingale* [nude] 8 x 5

Dainty, nymph-like nude reclining among sinuous vines against trunk of tree in shady glade, l. arm up, hand behind head, r. hand near waist, l. leg bent, the other straight. Bird perched on vine upper r. near margin. Dark. Monogram & © l. Cf. #63 *Pity's at the Pool*.

146 *Cornfield in Winter* 3½ x 6

Large, flat field, corn in shocks, all thinly blanketed with snow. Large, snowy tree and one small tree together r. of ctr. Other trees. Snow came from l. A few birds. Indistinct clouds. Monogram l. [Used by Burr as Christmas card, 1923. My copy: no title.]

147 *Warwick Castle from the Bridge* 6 x 8

Castle, half hidden by thick trees, stands above the Avon. White, solid-looking walls and several towers contrast with dark sky, dark foliage. Flag flying from crenelated tower r. of ctr. Billowing clouds. Water with reflections from below ctr. l. toward r. corner. Rowboats on shore, three figures, and a shed. Monogram & ⓒ l. [My copy: presentation copy dated 6/4/23; brown ink, dark gray paper.]

148 *Winter Snow* 3⅝ x 3⅝

Bare, snow-spotted trunks of two trees meet in Gothic arch over icy stream. Many irregular black dots sprinkled throughout. Both black and white reflect in dark stream low ctr. One tree standing straight on l., smaller one r. distance. Many horizontal lines in ice, fine horizontal lines in sky. Cold, wintry scene. Monogram r. [Used by Burr as Christmas card, 1917.]

149 *Brook in Winter* [no. 1] 3½ x 3½

Wintry scene. Group of five or six snow-spotted trees, the second from l. with corkscrew trunk. Icy stream, in shape of reversed number seven, goes around trees from ctr. to l., then to lower r. corner. Reflections ctr. to r. Snowy banks. Snow clings to many bushes in bgrd. Monogram l.

150 *Old Oaks* 10 x 7; 8 x 6

Oak tree ctr., some live, some dead branches. Smaller oak l. Split-rail fence on farther side of trees. Two small houses and trees in distance. Level terrain. Larger size: rock in r. fgrd. Monogram & ⓒ l. Smaller size: same description except plate cut above rock in fgrd. and on remaining three sides. Monogram alone l. For reproductions of both, see Chapter VII. [My copy (larger size): sepia; No. 3; Del. et Imp.; 1920; no title; not marked "trial proof."]

151 *Snow* 3½ x 3½

Small, wintry scene of trees and icy stream with damp, clinging snow. Shape of stream resembles back of r. hand, fingers curled under, wrist to r. Ground slopes from above ctr. l. to below ctr. r. Monogram l. Dark stream similar to #270 *First Snow* [no. 2] (q.v.).

152 *December* 3½ x 3½; 3½ x 6*

Wintry scene. Snow-spotted tree with thick, forked trunk l. of ctr., tops of two others near-by are beyond edge of plate. Snowy trees or bushes beyond. Black water low r. of ctr. to r. corner. Vertical lines in stream. Many black spots in wet, sticky snow. Ground rises from l. to r. Monogram l. [My copy: no title. Duplicate copy: Burr's signature r.; no title. Used by Burr as Christmas card, 1917.]

153 *March Snow* 5½ x 3½

Two snowy trees l. of ctr., three trees r. beside black, frozen pool with irregular outline ctr., several snow-covered mounds in it. Wet, clinging snow. Monogram l. Similar to #154 *Black Pool* (q.v.) and same size.

116

George Ellert Burr

Misty day Pauls Wharf London /03

FIGURE 43 — #276 *Misty Day, Pauls Wharf, London* 10 x 8 inches

154 *Black Pool* 5½ x 3½
Black, icy pool nearly fills ctr. lower third of plate. Two snow-spotted trees l. and one tree r., their trunks and the snowy banks mirrored in pool. Many fine, vertical lines in pool. Monogram l. This and #153 *March Snow* (q.v.) make an attractive pair. [My copy: penciled title on lower l. edge of bottom margin, not in Burr's handwriting.]

155 *The Range from Longmont, Colorado* 1¾ x 7
Cut from midde of #96 *Sketches near Longmont, Colorado* (q.v.). Entire skyline l. to r. is mtn. range, snow in a few ravines r. of ctr. Fgrd. is flat, fertile valley with groups of trees r. and l., three haystacks ctr. White mesa far l. Interesting contrast of dark and light. Monogram r. Cf. #156 *Longs Peak, Estes Park* [no. 3]. [Used by Burr as Christmas card, 1913.]

156 *Longs Peak, Estes Park* [no. 3] 1½ x 5
Except for added aquatint, identical with #24 *Longs Peak* [no. 1]. Cf. also #155 *The Range from Longmont, Colorado*, similar subject, somewhat similar size.

157 *Evening Cloud* [no. 1] 3 x 5; 2 x 3½
Exquisite miniature. In fgrd. sparsely wooded, steep mtn. slopes meeting r. of ctr. Larger slope on l. has prominent dead tree, a few live trees, their tops silhouetted against the sky. A distant view ctr. of plains and mesas beyond. Puffy white, sun-accented clouds above. Monogram r. Cf. #122 *Twilight* [no. 1].

158 *Autumn* [no. 2] 2 x 3½*
Have not found this etching.

159 *Broken Pine* 9½ x 7½
Mountain Moods series. One large tree with broken top, growing out of rocks. Two dead branches low r., others among live, leafy branches. Mtn. skyline, vicinity of Estes Park. Sky darkest at top, lightest through ctr. Monogram l. of ctr.

160 *Ragged Pine(s)* 9¾ x 7½
Mountain Moods series. This is found in two versions. NYPL copy: two large trees of irregular shape and ragged appearance. Tree on r. has dead fork hanging down on l. side of trunk about halfway to top; directly behind is small hemlock. Trunks grow out of pile of many rocks ctr. and r. fgrd. Low snow-covered mtns. l. form horizon; second from l. has snow-filled, star-shaped ravines or fissures. Monogram & © r. Denver Public Library copy (reproduced in the *Denver Times*, Mar. 30, 1916): a single large tree (the one on r. in version described above), and minor differences in details, although rocks and skyline are identical. Monogram alone r. Copy in Library of Congress has two pines; Fogg Art Museum, one.

161 *Brothers* 9¾ x 7½
Mountain Moods series. Two tall, slender trees l. of ctr. Trunk of taller one on l. slightly inclined toward r., its branches bent back toward smaller, straighter tree behind it, seemingly protecting it. Dark shadows directly underneath trees. Horizon of mtns., typical of Estes Park area, low on page. Snow in ravines r. Round clouds low and a few scattered puffs. Monogram r. [My copy: Trial Proof second state; Del. et Imp.; title at lower l. edge of bottom margin; G.E.B. ctr. lower margin.]

162   *Windswept Pine* [no. 3]   7½ x 9¾

Mountain Moods series. One large tree r. of ctr., trunk inclined to l., then curving r. near top. Longest branch of tree toward l. Clinging leaves, bare branches, some distorted and twisted. Sunlight from l. strikes trunk. Darkest shadows directly beneath tree. Snow caught in ravines of distant mtns. with tilting strata typical of Estes Park area. Streaks of light through sky. Monogram r.

163   *Moraine Park* [no. 1]   9¾ x 7½

Mountain Moods series. One solitary straight tree l. of ctr., dead top, dead lower branches, a few outcropping rocks near its roots. Mtns. in bgrd., near and far, tree-clad or bare. Cloud shadows. Monogram at base of tree l. of ctr. [Locale: Rocky Mountain National Park. My copy: no signature; no title; trial proof.]

164   *In Estes Park* [no. 1]   10 x 7

Mountain Moods series. Dark, pyramidal rock r., its point near ctr. In fgrd. l., a great pine, top out of picture, some low-growing plants. Longs Peak in distance far l. No clouds. Monogram l. Cf. #280 *Misty Moonlight, Estes Park, Colorado*, a reworked version.

165   *Windy Hill No. 6*   5½ x 3½; 4¾ x 3⅛

Two straight trees in ctr., tops bent to r. Two mtns. in bgrd. on lowest third of plate, snow in ravines, mtns. on r. snow-covered. Strong sunlight. Shadows to r. Streaks indicate rain or sleet from lower l. to upper r. Monogram l. [This etching and #166 *Windy Hill No. 7* (q.v.) were made on same plate and later separated. Both were cut to smaller sizes.]

166   *Windy Hill No. 7*   5½ x 3½; 3¾ x 3½

Full tree of irregular, ragged shape, trunk curving to r. at top. Triangular mtn. in far distance rising to point l. of ctr. A mtn. slope middle distance r. Low, white cloud puffs. Monogram r. Cf. #165 *Windy Hill No. 6*.

167   *Clear Creek Meadows, Denver* [no. 2]   4 x 7*

Have not found this etching. [This area figures also in #105 *Clear Creek Meadows, Denver* (no. 1) and #143 *The Range from Denver*.]

168   *The Leaning Pine*   8½ x 6½

Mountain Moods series. One large pine leaning gracefully from lower l. to upper r. Mtn. bgrd. l. to r. in lowest third of plate. Some snow on flat-topped mtn. r., snow between mtns. with tilting rock strata, typical of Estes Park area, their summits above timber line. Darkest mtns. in middle distance. One light spot in ctr. of dark sky shows off to advantage tree trunk, leaves, cones, dead branches. Monogram l. of ctr. [My copy: black and white; Del. et Imp.; no title. Duplicate copy: sepia; Del. et Imp.; no title.]

169   *Longs Peak, Moonlight*   6½ x 8½

Mountain Moods series. Majestic Longs Peak, snow in ravine, forms important interest with full moon r. of ctr. showing through drifting clouds. Tall pine growing among a few rocks fills r. third. Tree-clad lesser peaks in middle distance l. and beyond tree r. Dark. Monogram & © r.

170   *Mt. Chapin, Estes Park*   8½ x 6½   (see Fig. 25)

Mountain Moods series. Gently leaning pine tree with rocky foothold in fgrd. l. of ctr. allows view under its branches of Mt. Chapin in the Mummy Range, ctr., accented by moonlit snow on its flat top. Snow-clad ravines, gullies, crevices. Low-lying streaks of clouds. Rather dark tones, white accents. Some copies have monogram ctr., other copies no monogram.

171   *Bent Pine, Estes Park*   8½ x 6½

Mountain Moods series. Pine tree leans slightly to r. Trunk splits two-thirds up and forms letter *J*. Lower branches dead. Bgrd. consists of high-altitude view of mtns. typical of this area. Low clouds. Monogram r.

172   *Solitary Pine*   8½ x 6½

Mountain Moods series. One tall, slender tree r. of ctr. with pale trunk, growing out of many rocks on a high mtn. that slopes down to l. of ctr. Several leafless branches to r.; a dead, forked branch prominent on r. side of trunk. Speckled shadow on rock r. of trees. Top of white-tipped mtn. in distance lower than line of rocks in r. fgrd. Large rolling clouds, two small puffs alone, high l. of ctr. Monogram r. [My copy: title on bottom margin at l., not in Burr's handwriting.]

173   *Longs Peak, Morning, Estes Park*   6½ x 8½

Mountain Moods series. A dark mtn. scene. Longs Peak massif, gray, some snow in ravines, fills bgrd. A mtn. with flat top of vertical rock strata ctr. in middle distance has patches of round, dark trees on its slopes. Dark trees in fgrd. Boulders on edge of curving stream ctr. and r. Monogram l.

174   *Group of Pines, Estes Park*   8½ x 6½

Mountain Moods series. A solid, compact group of pines, the tallest in front and ctr., all making intricate shadows on large rock around which they stand. Pale, rocky summits low r. distance, with dusting of snow above timber line. Mtn. peak far distance l. Monogram l.

175   *Black Canyon, Estes Park*   8½ x 6½

Mountain Moods series. Dramatic upward sweep of mtn. slope r. distance to bare rocks with nearly vertical strata. A deep valley ctr. A small group of slender trees l., trunks accented by sunlight; the tops of two are lacy against sky. The l. bgrd. formed by steep mtn. slopes blanketed with dark trees and shade. Monogram l. [Black Canyon Creek flows in southerly direction past Bighorn Mountain and The Needles toward Estes Park Village.]

176   *Dead Pines, Estes Park*   8½ x 6½

Mountain Moods series. Two many-branched trees, tops broken off, standing l. of ctr. among rocks. Intricate and interesting pattern of branches with forked or stubby ends. Mtn. horizon low r., snow in ravines and canyons. Snow or rain streaks in sky. Monogram l.

177   *Skeleton Pine, Estes Park*   8½ x 6½

Mountain Moods series. One tree, leaning from ctr. to upper r., bizarre in appearance, could be either end up. No leaves. Scraggly branches silhouetted against light sky. Tree roots clutching rocks. Other rocks and small tree or leafy bushes r. of ctr. Slanted mountaintops in bgrd. Contrast of light and dark, dead and live branches. All shading darkest in ctr. Skyline almost exactly in ctr. Monogram r.

Figure 44 — #277 *Coast at Monterey, California*   10 x 8 inches

178 *Snow Storm, Estes Park*   6 x 7
Gracefully twisting tree r. of ctr. leaning l.; same curves repeated in four smaller trees under it, suggestive of parent leaning into storm, buffeted by the elements, protecting offspring. Snow on trunks, leaves, branches, rocks, and in sky. Fine sandpaper used for granular effect in background. Reminds one of Japanese art. Monogram & © l. Monogram & © (the latter reversed) partially obliterated lower r. corner. Cf. #225 *Brook in Winter* [no. 2].

179 *The Pine and the Cloud, Estes Park*   7 x 6
Tall, straight pine tree l. of ctr. To its r. the edge of a large cottony cloud repeats its outline. Trunk of tree is mottled by strong sunlight. A number of dead branches, others with leaves. Rocks scattered near its base l. of ctr. fgrd. A group of about eight very ordinary trees just beyond on level ground. To r. a deep valley is suggested by dark tree-covered mtn. slope in middle distance r. Snowy mtns. rising beyond and forming skyline. Many clouds. Monogram & © l.

180 *Pines in Wind, Estes Park*   6 x 7   (see Fig. 36)
From lower r. to upper l., two contorted and windblown trees with pale, skeletal trunks, growing side by side at timber line, trunks and branches swept hard to l. Mtn. peaks far distance low l. White, turbulent clouds, rain streaks throughout sky. Monogram & ©, both upside down, r. [My copy: no title.]

181 *Moraine Park, Estes Park, Colorado* [no. 2]   5 x 3½
Thick trunk and lower branches of sturdy pine l. of ctr., with a profusion of leaves and cones l., top, and r., frame distant view of sharp-pointed peak with snowy ravines. Under foot, rocks, bushes, and grass. Viewer is drawn into picture. Monogram & © l. [When used as frontispiece in *The Print Connoisseur*, I (June 1921), neither the artist's signature nor the title appear on lower margin.]

182 *Rhône Valley*   3 x 4
Setting sun r. of ctr. illumines sky, backlighting clouds, silhouetting sharp-pointed trees and haystacks ctr., and shining on trunk of round, pollarded tree l. Mtns. in distance l. and r. Reflections in water fgrd. No monogram discernible in finished state. [Used by Burr as Christmas card, 1920.]

183 This number is unaccountably passed over in both *The Print Connoisseur* "Catalogue Raisonné" and American Etchers series, Vol. VII. To the best of my knowledge, no etching was so numbered.

184 *Arizona Clouds* [no. 2]   7 x 10
Desert Set — the first title in this series; in black and white, from reworked plate of #68 *Arizona Clouds* [no. 1] (q.v.), the only mezzotint Burr ever made. Thick, rolling clouds, caught in sunlight above dark and dense clouds in vast sky, are more prominent than in color version. Rocker or roulette marks in light areas can be seen in some copies. Monogram r. [Each of the thirty-five titles in the Desert Set bears its own number penciled in the lower margin at r. (see Chapter III).]

185 *Near Gallup*   3 x 5*
Have not found this etching. [#210 *Navajo Church, New Mexico* and #272 *Pyramid Mountain, New Mexico* were also made in this scenic area.]

186 *Yuccas*   7 x 4½; 6¾ x 5; 6¾ x 4½; 7¾ x 4½*
Desert Set. A group of large yuccas, typical of the Southwest, stands r. of ctr., four others grouped middle distance l. Sparse vegetation, heavy shadows to r. Mtns. in far distance. Low horizon. Great detail, sharp contrast. Monogram l.

187 *Desert Night*   9¾ x 7½
Desert Set. Dark scene with full moon upper l. quadrant. One sharp peak in distance l. of ctr., a more distant mtn. extreme l. Moonlight reflects on flat-topped mtn. r. middle distance, other mtns. in front of it. Fgrd. consists of perfectly flat desert floor with sparse vegetation entire l. to r. Monogram & © l. Somewhat similar to #314 *Arizona Night* (q.v.).

188 *Joshua Trees*   7 x 5; 8 x 5*
Scattered group of angular, grotesque Joshua trees ("giant" yuccas) in fgrd., their sharp-pointed leaves growing in clumps. Small desert plants around them, shadows to l. Low mtn. skyline, dark and sawtoothed. Monogram l. [Burr's note on NYPL trial proof: "Plate destroyed, no prints."]

189 *Sandstorm on the Little Colorado River*   6¾ x 9¾
Desert Set. Color etching. A dramatic soft-ground representation of violent sandstorm. Heavy streaks slanting downward from upper l. to far r. almost obliterating buttes in ctr. Group of trees l. in middle distance. Small shrubs on waves of sand. Monogram & © l.

190 *Near Kingman, Arizona*   6¼ x 9½
Desert Set. Desert mesas and buttes in middle distance entire l. to r.; bgrd. of dark, pointed mtns. Herd of cattle, low-growing bushes and shrubs in fgrd. Rain streaks and clouds over all, heaviest on l. Monogram & © l. Cf. #207 *Near Lamy, New Mexico* [no. 2]. [My copy: light orange-brown ink; No. 26/40; no title; G.E.B. lower r.]

191 *Soapweed* [no. 1]   7 x 5
Desert Set. A beautiful desert yucca in full bloom with one tall and two shorter spikes of hanging, bell-shaped, white blossoms against slightly darkened bgrd. Low, sharp leaves. Monogram & © l. Cf. #286 *Soapweed, Arizona* [no. 2].

192 *Palm Canyon* [no. 1]   7 x 5
Desert Set. One lone palm tree r. of ctr. standing at bottom of steep, rocky canyon. Sparse vegetation at base of tree, all else stark, barren canyon walls. Heavy drypoint l. Monogram l. Cf. #331 *Palm Canyon Plate 2*, an enlarged version. [My copy: Trial Proof; Del. et Imp.]

193 *Santa Catalina Mountains, Tucson, Arizona*   5 x 8
Desert Set. Spacious desert landscape, dark flora on white sand making pleasing contrast with long ridge of pale mtns. in distance l. to r. Cloudless sky. Monogram & © l.

194 *A Mirage* [no. 1]   7 x 10   (see Fig. 26)
Desert Set. Through ctr. a mirage of beautiful lake reflecting mtns. in middle distance. Pale, tall mtns. form bgrd. Sparse vegetation in fgrd. Ethereal quality and great delicacy. Monogram l. Not to be confused with #287 *A Mirage, Ari-*

zona [no. 2] (q.v.). [My copy: Trial Proof No. 3; Del. et Imp.; no title; G.E.B. in yellow crayon.]

195 *Oasis of Seven Palms, California* 5 x 7

Desert Set. Nearly straight horizontal line of dark palm trees standing on desert terrain with spotty vegetation. The San Jacinto Mountains, pale and delicate with soft shadows, stand majestically in bgrd., skyline repeating top outline of trees. Much contrast. Monogram & © l.

196 *Drifting Sand near Amboy, California* 6 x 7

Desert Set. Sharp, jagged, dark edges of mtns. emerging from vast expanse of pale, windswept sand; two large peaks r. and l. bgrd. Low fgrd. l., two riders heading l. Low r., cluster of dark desert plants with dagger-like leaves. Monogram & © r.

197 *Whirlwinds, Mojave Desert* [no. 1] 5 x 7 (see Fig. 37)

Desert Set. Dark, jagged mtn. range in bgrd. entire l. to r., white sand caught in ravines. Three delicate whirlwinds ctr. middle distance rising from flat, white, desert floor and making shadows to l. A fourth appears in early trial proofs. Fgrd. spotted with small, dark clumps of vegetation. Finely executed. Monogram & © r. Cf. #281 *Whirlwinds, Dead Mountains, Mojave Desert, California* [no. 2] and #312 *Whirlwinds* [no. 3]. [My copy: title on bottom margin at l., not in Burr's handwriting; Trial Proof /40.]

198 *Prickly Pear Cactus* 7¼ x 5

Desert Set. Cactus with spines and flat saucer-like leaves minutely portrayed, branching up and out from low ctr. Heavy shadows immediately beneath. Number of blossoms on edges of leaves varies with individual prints, thus emphasizing, whether intentional on Burr's part or not, their ephemeral appeal. No bgrd. Monogram & © l. [My copy: palest green paper; No. 12/40; two blossoms, two buds. Copy in Oklahoma Art Center: No. 18/40, six blossoms, four buds.]

199 *Desert Dunes* [no. 1] 5 x 7

Desert Set. No mtn. bgrd. Masses of undulating white sand spotted with scrub trees and bushes, largest l. of ctr. fgrd. Shadows to lower r. Remarkably delicate. Monogram & © r. Easily confused with #323 *Dunes near Palm Springs, California* [no. 2] (q.v.).

200 *Cholla Cactus* 8 x 5

Desert Set. Color etching. Profusely needled cactus in great detail with sharp, dark shadows in lattice pattern beneath and r. Butte in bgrd. l., pointed mtn. r. Small trees and shrubs. Monogram & © l. Most copies in black and white. A very few, whose coloring ranges from palest greens and blues to delicate brown, might be considered experimental.

201 *Palo Verde Trees* 5 x 7

Desert Set. Two round, full trees ctr. Dark mtns. in bgrd. Important round, swirling clouds. Soft ground in sepia gives crayon-like effect. Monogram & © l. [My copy: Del. et Imp.; no title; Trial Proof. Duplicate copy: no title; red ink; No. 7/40.]

George Elbert Burr

Evening – Paradise Valley – Arizona –

FIGURE 45 — #282 *Evening, Paradise Valley, Arizona*   8 x 10 inches

202   *Palm Springs, California*   5¼ x 7

Desert Set. Log house labeled "BATH" with gable and shuttered windows, almost surrounded by tall palms. Partial view of trees r. casting long shadows on open spaces of roadway ctr. to r. Details fade toward edges. Monogram l., with or without ©. [My copy: has title; Trial Proof /40.]

203   *Twilight, Laguna, New Mexico* [no. 2]   5 x 8

Desert Set. Dark and mysterious desert landscape. Large clouds drifting far l. and r., largest in ctr. caught in afterglow. Distant horizon of arid mtns. Desert floor scarcely visible. Monogram l. Cf. #318 *Desert Twilight.*

204   *Ocotillo* [no. 1]   8 x 5*

Have not found this etching. [When in bloom, the long, slender stems of this thorny plant, each bearing bright red blossoms at the end, resemble whips with red tassels, whence the popular name "Coach (or Buggy) Whip."]

205   *Barrel Cactus* [no. 1]   5 x 8

Desert Set. R. of ctr. a barrel cactus and ocotillo in bloom, its blossomy stems spread against the sky. A smaller barrel cactus with curved ribs, buds on its top, ctr. Scattered small desert flora. Eroded desert mtn. l. Monogram & © l. of ctr. Easily confused with #288 *Barrel Cactus* [no. 2] (q.v.).

206   *Giant Cactus*   8 x 6

Desert Set. Many tall saguaros, some branched, some not, solemnly standing on mountainside that gently slopes down from r. to l., leading the eye to pointed mtns. in far l. distance. Other desert flora. Shadows toward l. Monogram & © r. [My copy: palest yellow paper.]

207   *Near Lamy, New Mexico* [no. 2]   10 x 7

Desert Set. Many varieties of desert flora ctr. fgrd. on either side of arroyo leading down into vast grazing lands. Mesas in distance. Dark and pointed mtns. form bgrd. Large bank of cumulus clouds; cloud streaks near mountaintops. Monogram & © l. Cf. #190 *Near Kingman, Arizona.*

208   *Moonlight, Holbrook, Arizona*   5 x 8

Desert Set. Dark landscape. Romantic effect of full moon l. of ctr. backlighting clouds, silvering their edges. Desert-like floor catches some light. Dark mtns. in distance. No monogram.

209   *Black Mesa*   4 x 6*

Have not found this etching. [There are Black Mesas in northern Arizona, northern New Mexico, and southern Colorado.]

210   *Navajo Church, New Mexico*   7 x 5   (see Fig. 27)

Desert Set. Extremely delicate and fine-lined portrayal of odd-shaped rock formation (now called Church Rock) near Gallup, standing atop other eroded rocks. Sheer rock wall beneath falls away and etching fades to edges. Leafy branches of tree r. of ctr. near base line. Monogram & © l. [My copy: Trial Proof No. 2; Del. et Imp.; no monogram; title lower l. edge of bottom margin, not in Burr's handwriting.]

211 *Needles Mountains, Colorado River, Arizona* 9½ x 12

Desert Set. Formidable, grotesque, jagged mtn. peaks form bgrd. above placid bend of Colorado River, rounded trees and bushes along its banks. Drypoint streaks in fgrd. Monogram & © r. [Locale: Mojave Mountains near Topock. My copy: Del. et Imp.; has title; Trial Proof /40.]

212 *Grand Canyon* [no. 1]   12 x 10   (see Fig. 28)

Desert Set. Bold and striking portrayal of canyon, executed in soft ground. Monogram & © l. See #275 *Canyon Rim, Arizona;* also #330 *Grand Canyon Plate 3.* [My copy: No. 14/40; Del. et Imp.; title lower l. corner of margin. Awarded first prize for etchings at Arizona State Fair according to *Art News,* XXIII (Nov. 29, 1924), 8.]

213 *Cloudburst*   10 x 12

Desert Set. Landscape partially obscured by rain streaks and heavy, dark clouds on r. Bright sky ctr. Rounded clouds hang low in ctr. and l. Mtns. emerge in bright sunlight ctr. and l. bgrd. Spots of reflected light on flat desert-like floor. No trees or vegetation of any kind. Monogram & © l. Cf. #220 *Desert Shower.* Similar, except for size, to #93 *From My Cabin Window.*

214 *From Indio, California*   10 x 12

Desert Set. Color etching. Ethereal landscape. Morning haze and mist, typical of this area near Salton Sea, lie between desert floor, with spots of vegetation in fgrd., and mtns. in bgrd. Snow-capped summit ctr. Great delicacy suggests Japanese print. Monogram & © l. Only a very limited number in color. Some copies in palest colors, others in pale monochrome. [My copy: gray ink; No. 21/40; Del. et Imp.; no title.]

215 *Evening Cloud* [no. 2]   12 x 10

Desert Set. Tranquil, rather dark landscape. Large, luminous white cloud in vast expanse of sky dominates scene below. Distant mtns., highest in ctr. Interesting light and shadow on mtns. and plains. Spots of shrubs lower l. Monogram & © l.

216 *Mesa Encantada, New Mexico* [no. 1]   6 x 8

Desert Set. Extremely delicate, fine-lined portrayal of lone mesa in shades of gray. Cumulus and strato-cumulus clouds above, highest l. of ctr. Spots of vegetation in fgrd., small bush extreme lower l. corner. Impressions from this plate are more delicate than those from #320 *Mesa Encantada, New Mexico* [no. 2] (q.v.), with which it is sometimes confused. Monogram & © r. [My copy: trial proof on rice paper; no title or other label to identify it with the Desert Set.]

217 *Piñon Trees*   10 x 12

Desert Set. Dark pine with thick, forked trunk l. Gracefully leaning white tree trunks ctr. Above, high-piled white clouds like cotton balls in dark sky. Mtns. and mesas, bgrd. l. to r., mostly sunlit. Rain streaks far r. " '20" in r. corner of plate. Monogram & © r. This and #227 *Old Cedars and Spanish Peaks, Colorado* make a congenial pair. Cf. #333 *Desert Clouds.* [My copy: No. 37/40; no title.]

218 *Old Cedars, New Mexico*   10 x 12

Desert Set. Gnarled and stunted old cedars leaning l. from r. corner. Long branches lying on ground, joining other tangled trees lower l. Convolutions of twisted growths and many leaves in great detail. Beyond is glimpse of flat desertland and mtn. bgrd. Clouds low in sky suggested in simple outline. "'20" on plate r. of ctr. Monogram & © r. of ctr. Cf. #317 *Old Cedar, Ash Fork, Arizona*. [My copy: No. 19/40; Del. et Imp.; no title.]

219   *Death Valley*   5 x 8*

Have not found this etching.

220   *Desert Shower*   7 x 10

Desert Set. Dark, turbulent rain clouds dominate upper r.; below, distant mtns., bright sky, shadings of light on the plains. Rain streaks entire l. to r. Thick grouping of trees l. fgrd., white trunk and branches contrasting with dark mass. Spotty vegetation r. middle distance. Dramatic. Monogram & © l. Cf. #213 *Cloudburst*.

221   *Sunset*   7 x 10

Desert Set. Grand vista above timber line. Rugged and barren mtns., those ctr. and l. in shadow, those on r. and deep valley in fgrd. still distinguishable in last light of setting sun just sunk from sight l. of ctr. Sketchy cumulus clouds and shafts of light in sky. Monogram & © l. [Some copies on pale pink paper. My copy: No. 19/40; Del. et Imp.; title lower l. edge of lower margin.]

222   *San Francisco Mountains, Arizona* [no. 1]   7 x 10

Desert Set. Color etching. Delicate, fine-lined interpretation of these massive and impressive mtns. near Flagstaff. Snow in highest ravines blending into misty sky. Darker foothills. Flat, arid tableland fgrd. dotted by a few trees and shrubs, mostly at extreme r. Clouds and rain streaks on r. Monogram & © l. A very few, delicate and subtle, in color. Cf. #339 *San Francisco Peaks, Arizona* [no. 2], slightly larger. [My copy: pale green ink; No. 7/40; Del. et Imp.; no title.]

223   *Dawn in the Land of the Buttes*   6 x 8

Desert Set. Delicate, sensitive landscape of lonely, weatherbeaten, disintegrating buttes standing in sandy wastelands. Meager vegetation lower l. only. Shadings of gray. Pale, ethereal. Monogram & © l. [My copy: pale greenish-gray ink; No. 26/40; Del. et Imp.; no title.]

224   *November*   7½ x 6

Peaceful rural landscape of fields and trees, rolling farmland. In fgrd. two large, leafless trees with many branches; between them l. to r. a stake-and-rider fence with break in ctr. Bright sky affords strong contrast and suggests that sun has just gone down. In some impressions heavy inking obscures details easily seen in lighter ones. Monogram & © l.

225   *Brook in Winter* [no. 2]   7½ x 6

Wintry scene with cold, wet snow. Tree l. of icy stream in which are snow-covered rocks, etc. Forked tree r., many branches intertwined. A few shrubs. Reflections in ice fgrd. Some contrast, but grayness predominates. Monogram & © l. Cf. #178 *Snow Storm, Estes Park*.

226   *Pikes Peak, Colorado*   12 x 10

Snow-covered Pikes Peak forms skyline from l. to beyond ctr. r. Straight, slender tree r. of ctr. growing out of clefts in huge boulders at timber line, its trunk in light, its top against dark and threatening sky. One stubby, broken-off branch to r., one leafy branch up, several branches to l. Steep, sparsely timbered mtn.

slope, with light snow, descends sharply in l. fgrd. Dark tops of lesser peaks without snow and at lower altitude are in middle distance ctr. and l. Two birds l. distinguishable in some prints, not in others. "1922" in r. corner on plate. Monogram & Ⓒ r. Not to be confused with #59 *Old Cedar and Pikes Peak* (q.v.).

227 *Old Cedars and Spanish Peaks, Colorado* 10 x 12

Stunted, low-spreading trees growing amid rocks r. fgrd. Flat desert-like terrain beyond, a few trees in middle distance, mesas l. Two similar, pointed peaks l. of ctr. in distance not prominent as they blend into clouds. One bright cloud r. of ctr. behind top of tree. Dark sky, slanting rain streaks l. Many lines. "1922" in r. corner on plate. Monogram & Ⓒ r. Cf. #138 *Spanish Peaks* [no. 2], in color, same size. [This etching and #217 *Piñon Trees*, both in black and white and the same size, make a congenial pair. My copy: Second State; Trial Proof No. 4; Del. et Imp.; no title.]

228 *Timberline Storm* 10 x 12

White cloud ctr. behind storm-tossed trees leaning to l. Strong exposed roots, rocks in fgrd. Distant mtns. l. with many white patches. Dark sky full of rain streaks. Dark clouds on r. Storm from upper r. Dramatic. An extraordinary number of lines. "1922" on plate r. Monogram & Ⓒ r. Cf. #139 *Home of the Winds* [no. 2].

229 *Bear Creek Canyon, Denver, Colorado* 12 x 10

Deep, awesome canyon between mtn. walls of tilted rock strata. Light and shadow, sunlight and shade. Trees in ctr. fgrd. growing beside Bear Creek. On path l. of ctr. two figures, one on horseback. Sketchy clouds l. "1922" on plate r. corner. Monogram & Ⓒ r.

230 *Old Pine, Estes Park, Colorado* 12 x 10

Straight trunk, its bark etched in great detail, and some branches of mighty tree l. of ctr., dead branches prominent against sky. Open valley; two figures on horseback heading r. can be seen low in middle distance. In far distance important mtns. form low skyline. Viewer seems drawn into picture. Monogram & Ⓒ r. [My copy: title on lower l. edge of bottom margin, not in Burr's handwriting.]

231 *Village Street, Lake Lugano, Italy* [no. 1] 12 x 10

Female figure holding feather duster, hands at waist, standing in large, dark, arched doorway in stone building r. of ctr. Above, a rectangular window with open shutters. Thick stem of tall vine ctr. and two supporting poles, many leaves on horizontal trellis casting shadows down and to r. Path leads from doorway to low ctr., then turns l. and reverses direction, continuing to descend past house with tile roof and small open archway through which is seen a pointed tree. Capped chimney above tile roof l. outlined against lake with small craft and reflections. Mtn. bgrd. Details fade toward edges. On plate r.: "192[2?]," monogram & Ⓒ. Cf. #285 *On Lake Lugano, Italy* [no. 2], a cut version of this; also #349 *Lake Lugano, Italy* [no. 3].

232 *Old Pines near Timberline* 8½ x 6½

Broken, tangled trees standing ctr. and r., some dead, some live. Two dead trunks horizontal on ground l. and ctr. among grasses and rocks. Mtn. skyline l. distance. Design forms letter *A*. Monogram & Ⓒ l.

233 *Old Pine and Cedar* 9¾ x 7⅜
Tangle of trees growing out of rocks in W pattern, tallest pine in ctr. Much detail of pine leaves, bark, dead branches. Mtn. far r. Monogram & © ctr.

234 *Near Monterey* 3½ x 5
Two trees with pale trunks and dark leaves, one l. and one r. of ctr., leaning together and mingling branches. Most branches windblown l. Small tree, bushes l. in bgrd. Rocky coast. Low horizon. Water (Pacific Ocean) beyond trees, boat on horizon r. of ctr. trailing smoke to l. Monogram & © l.

235 *Old Cypress near Monterey* 5 x 3½
Large, decorative tree, lower branches dead and stubby, standing r. of ctr. among rocks on seacoast. Water and mtns. in distance visible l. to r. Billowing white clouds through ctr. Birds in sky l. Monogram & © r. See #277 *Coast at Monterey, California,* a similar subject but different size. [Used by Burr as Christmas card, 1922.]

236 *[Christmas Plate]* [no. 1] 3½ x 5
Limber pine with dark trunk and strong roots l. of ctr., windswept to r. Other trees with white trunks, lower middle distance r. White mtn. peaks far distance r. Monogram & © l. Easily confused with #237 *[Christmas Plate]* [no. 2] (q.v.). [My copy: printed on half of folder; on other half in pencil, "The Seasons Greetings from George E. Burr. Dec. 1923"; no title.]

237 *[Christmas Plate]* [no. 2] 3½ x 5
Tree has light trunk and is inclined at sharper angle than in #236. On l. are small trees and white mtn. peak in distance. Monogram & © r. Easily confused with #236 *[Christmas Plate]* [no. 1] (q.v.). The two make an agreeable pair. [My copy: folder torn in half, remaining sheet intact; no title; no date.]

238 *Road in the Campagna, Rome* 5 x 7
An arid landscape. Trees of various shapes, bushes, etc., casting shadows to l. on road ctr. fgrd. to distance. Two figures on road, one seated, one standing. Rude fence l. corner, wire fence with posts r. Ruins of Roman aqueduct l. in middle distance. Mtn. bgrd. A few birds in sky r. "ROME" on plate r. Monogram & © l. Cf. #248 *From Appian Way, Rome,* a pastoral scene in same general area. [For locale see #3 *The Campagna.*]

239 *Mouth of the Arno* 6 x 9
Row of separate shacks built on pilings, nets hanging on drying frames. Beyond to r., water and houses. In fgrd., grasses pushing up through sand; r. a solitary fisherman. A few low clouds, birds. Mtns. far distance. Fine lines, delicate. Title etched on plate l. Monogram r. [The Arno empties into the Ligurian Sea a few miles north of Leghorn (Livorno).]

240 *Ventimiglia, Italy* 7 x 10
Many tall, solid-looking houses built on far side of steeply rising river bank in oldest part of this city on the Costa dei Fiori. Three female figures l. fgrd., two kneeling at low river's edge, doing a washing. Two trees l. and an arched bridge over river far l. middle distance. The high Maritime Alps form bgrd. Threatening sky. Monogram r. [My copy: presentation copy; inscription erased, but "12/25/31" still discernible; no title. See #52 *Heidelberg, Sunset* and footnote listing other bridges.]

FIGURE 46 — #286 *Soapweed, Arizona* [no. 2]   10 x 7 inches

Courtesy of the Cincinnati Art Museum

241 *Florence from Fiesole* 5¾ x 9
View overlooking roofs of Florence with Cathedral, Baptistry, and Campanile easily identifiable. Dark, shapeless rainclouds, typical of Arno valley, casting dark shadows on city. In fgrd. suggestion of many trees; house and cypress trees low r. of ctr. Surrounding hills rising gently in bgrd. Monogram l. of ctr.

242 *Florence from Monte Oliveto* [no. 2]   12 x 10
A stately olive tree dominates fgrd., its exposed roots prominent in l. corner. In angle formed by its leaning trunk and the olive orchard (Ital. *oliveto*) descending the slopes of the hill are seen a compact grouping of many-windowed buildings and, in ctr., the Cathedral, Baptistry, and Campanile. Other domes rise above roofs. Low mtns. beyond l. to r. Low rolling clouds. Monogram r. On trial proof: "1931" on plate r.; monogram r. Cf. #39 *Florence from Monte Oliveto* [no. 1], a color etching and smaller size. See also #346 *Florence from Monte Oliveto* [no. 3].

243 *Bordighera, Italy* 7 x 10*
Have not found this etching. [Bordighera is on the Italian Riviera near French frontier. Like other towns in vicinity, it has ancient section, beautiful gardens, view of the Mediterranean from high vantage points.]

244 *Rome from Tivoli* 7 x 10
Rustic scene looking toward Rome from Alban Hills. Olive trees with unusual trunks, some with tripod-like roots above ground, entire l. to r. fgrd. on hillside. Meandering road ctr., rolling fields, scattered dwellings. Picnickers, umbrella, two donkeys r. fgrd. Rome and St. Peter's in distance. Monogram l. [My copy: no title. Burr's note on NYPL copy: "Trial Proof final state 10/24/1927."]

245 *Capri from Sorrento* 10 x 7   (see Fig. 38)
Dark, misty night scene, thick clouds with full moon l. of ctr. Moonlight reflected in water l. Three tall stone pines, tallest on l. Other trees forming bgrd. in middle distance near edge of water. Isle of Capri in distance blending into bgrd l. to r. No monogram. Cf. #350 *Stone Pines near Sorrento, Italy.*

246 *Venice after Storm* 10 x 12
Stern view of three large, dark fishing boats r. of ctr. lying at anchor, nets hanging from masts. Figures in boats. Two white churches (Santa Maria della Salute and San Giorgio Maggiore) l. of ctr. in sun and beautifully reflected in water. Low, puffy clouds. Rain slanting from upper l. Birds in sky. A few small craft. Atmospheric condition superbly portrayed. Monogram l. Cf. #75 *Venetian Fishing Boats.*

247 *From French Academy, Rome* 5 x 8
Round, shallow, footed basin with splashing fountain. Two gracefully arching trees meet overhead and afford view of St. Peter's and buildings of Rome. On r. two priests walking toward l. on path beside fountain and next to low wall running entire l. to r. Dark, shady fgrd. Monogram l. [Viewer stands before the Accademia Francese in the Villa Medici. Not visible are, at his r., the beautiful gardens, and, at his l., the church Santa Trinità dei Monti.]

248 *From Appian Way, Rome* 6 x 9; 5 x 8*   (see Fig. 39)
Ruins of ancient aqueduct in middle distance entire l. to r. In fgrd. r. two stone pines, their umbrella-like tops against the sky. Uneven ground. At l. a shepherd

driving his sheep, possibly toward pasturage in the Apennines which form bgrd. A few trees l. The use of drypoint and blank areas suggests strong sunlight. Monogram l. Cf. #238 *Road in the Campagna, Rome,* a pastoral scene in same general area. [My copy: no title; trial proof.]

249   *Old Olive and Monte Carlo*   10 x 12

Ancient, huge olive tree, many twisted trunks and contorted roots filling almost entire area. Glimpse of water r. and Monte Carlo basking in sun, sheltered by mtns. rising from coast. All impressions I have seen are dark, with heavy inking. [My copy: no monogram.]

250   *Superstition Mountain, Apache Trail, Arizona* [no. 1]   7 x 10

Angular, rocky, eroded mtn. is centered on plate, emphasizing its foreboding and unfriendly character. Dark clouds above cast shadows on middle distance. Mtn. and fgrd. in sunlight. Giant and other varieties of cactus scattered on desert floor in fgrd. Rain streaks and swirling clouds add a fitting mood to this region of legends and insidious hazards. Monogram & © r. See #325 *Superstition Mountain, Apache Trail, Arizona, Night* [no. 2].

251   *Near Echo Canyon, Phoenix, Arizona*   10 x 7

Prominent on l., a many-branched saguaro; ocotillo, barrel cactus, etc., shrubs and small trees. Eroded mtn. in bgrd. rises high r. of ctr. Threatening sky. Dark, strong shadows. Monogram & © l.

252   *Indian Homes, Gila River, Arizona*   5 x 7

A small house standing in desert l. of ctr.; it has one window, one small, low doorway; shaded area r. under extended roof made of branches. Two figures in shade, one standing, one seated. Baskets, pottery jars, a few chickens, a dog. Several long pieces of wood lying on ground l., one with axe in it. Another house far l. Spotty vegetation. Estrella Mountains form skyline r. and far distance l. Clouds. A few birds r. Monogram & © l. [Burr's photograph of this spot (in my possession) bears his notation "Near St. John's Mission."]

253   *Road to Paradise Valley, Arizona*   5¼ x 7¼

Desert landscape with bare, curving road from ctr. to r., then to lower l. Many-branched saguaros standing like sentinels among low-growing cacti, etc., in expanse of sand. Pointed mtn. (Camelback) r. bgrd.; others on horizon l. and r. Monogram & © l. [A better-known view of this mtn. is seen in #255 *Camelback Mountain, Phoenix, Arizona.*]

254   *Arizona Canal, Phoenix*   6 x 9

Canal with grassy banks l. to r., reflecting trees that grow on far side. A beautiful, reposeful landscape. McDowell Mountains form skyline. Round, puffy clouds thick r. of ctr. On plate r.: "PHOENIX," monogram & ©. [Copyrighted 1926 under title *Grand Canal, Phoenix, Evening.* Both canals go through Phoenix.]

255   *Camelback Mountain, Phoenix, Arizona*   7 x 10

Landscape with mtn. skyline resembling camel's back, head to l. A few sketchy clouds. One prominent saguaro with four arms fgrd. r.; others scattered among variety of cacti and bushes in middle distance. Cloud shadows through ctr. Monogram & © l.

256 *Arizona Storm*   4½ x 6

Barren desert landscape — no trees, no vegetation. Sky full of stormy clouds boldly portrayed with many lines. Desert butte in sun, fgrd. Mtns. far r. and ctr. distance. Monogram & © r. Cf. #258 *Storm in the Painted Desert, Arizona;* #260 *Storm on the Little Colorado River, Arizona.* Although #269 *Evening, Painted Desert, Arizona* (q.v.) does not depict a storm, it is similar. [My copy: no title.]

257 *The Little Canyon*   6 x 4½

Large, block-like rock walls rising r. and l. with glimpse ctr. of level desert floor. Flat eroded butte ctr. distance. Billowing clouds. No vegetation. Barren. Monogram l. [Plate steel-faced to permit large printing of frontispiece for *The Print Connoisseur,* X (Oct. 1930), which lacks usual artist's penciled signature in lower l. margin. My copy: signature l.; "The Seasons greetings from George Elbert Burr 12/25/27." Duplicate copy (probably from the magazine): no signature; no title.]

258 *Storm in the Painted Desert, Arizona*   4½ x 6

Dark, stormy sky with heavy clouds and rain streaks, light spot r. of ctr. Clump of trees l. fgrd. Ground slopes down from both l. and r. Light shines on butte in middle distance and on flat desert floor. Pointed mtn. far distance r. Monogram & © l. Cf. #256 *Arizona Storm* and #260 *Storm on the Little Colorado River, Arizona.*

259 *San Xavier Mission, Tucson, Arizona*   7 x 10

Gleaming white in desert sun, this splendid example of Spanish Renaissance architecture is fittingly called the "White Dove of the Desert." Two towers, the one on r. without a dome, an ornate façade made partly of adobe, a long wall with pierced trim extending toward r. At r. a man and two women, a horse tied to tree. Small trees on both sides of wall. Exquisite detail. Monogram & © l. [The Mission of San Xavier del Bac (founded before 1700, present building erected before 1800) is southwest of Tucson.]

260 *Storm on the Little Colorado River, Arizona*   4½ x 6

Dark, stormy sky over desert landscape. Trees in l. and r. corners. Heavy shadows fall toward l., slanting rain middle distance l. and r. Bright sky ctr. Sunshine on large eroded mtn. Other mtns. on horizon. Monogram & © l. Cf. #256 *Arizona Storm* and #258 *Storm in the Painted Desert, Arizona.*

261 *Estrella Mountains, Gila River, Arizona*   5 x 7

High, sharp-pointed mtns. l. descending to placid, shallow-appearing river in flat area. Eroded banks r. Some trees. In fgrd. clumps of grasses, some dead wood. Monogram & © l. [At this point the Gila River flows between the Sierra Estrella and the Salt River Mountains. The Salt River joins it near-by, west and south of Phoenix.]

262 *The Desert, Arizona* [no. 2]   6 x 8

Black-and-white version, in a larger edition, of #102 *The Desert* [no. 1] (q.v.). Plate cut. Slight reworking. Monogram & © r. [Added (1928) to permanent collection in Bibliothèque Nationale.]

263 *Desert Sentinels, Apache Trail, Arizona* 5 x 7½

Factual representation of desert life. Three old saguaros in fgrd. showing nesting holes made by desert birds. Other giant cacti and many smaller varieties growing on flat floor, from fgrd. toward large Superstition Range which fills bgrd. Cloudless sky. Monogram & © l.

264 *Fish Creek, Apache Trail, Arizona* 6⅝ x 4⅞; 6⅝ x 4 (see Fig. 40)

Deep V-shaped canyon, a small creek r. of ctr. between steep, rocky walls. Flat, nearly horizontal surfaces of rocks fgrd. l. of ctr. Study in full range of shadings. No clouds. No trees. Monogram r. Easily confused with #298 *Sketch on Apache Trail, Arizona* (q.v.). Wider size, a trial proof, has remarque at l., full length of plate and ⅞″ wide, consisting of cartoon figures: top to bottom, man with arms extended and halo above head; head and torso of man with glasses (presumably a self-caricature); "I DID IT," with Burr's monogram beneath; face of woman with glasses and large hair-bow against dark bgrd., "7/8/26" beneath; profile of woman's face, white against black bgrd., looking down to r. This same profile appears hidden in edges of rocks about 1″ from top r. — a humorous device used in children's picture puzzles. [My copy (smaller size): "George Elbert Burr 12/25/26." Duplicate copy has aquatint and full moon; no signature; no title.]

265 *Summer Cloud, Apache Trail, Arizona* 8 x 10; 10 x 12*

Strong contrasts. White, billowing cloud mass; highest in ctr. has almost same outline as graceful, delicate, thickly leaved trees and bushes growing out of rock fissures r. ctr. Inclined rocky ledges fgrd., accented in heavy drypoint. Eroded, angular mtns. lower l. in far distance. Monogram r. Not to be confused with #334 *Evening on the Little Colorado River*.

266 *Moonlight, Phoenix, Arizona* 3½ x 5⅜; 3½ x 5

Dark print with full moon upper r. backlighting clouds over summit of mtn. (Camelback). Saguaro and ocotillo among other varieties of desert flora. Curving Arizona Canal reflects light. No monogram.

267 *A New England Road* [no. 2] 5 x 8

This is #66 *A New England Road* [no. 1] (q.v.) trimmed to smaller size and reworked. Same description. No monogram.

268 *Cloud Shadows, Apache Trail, Arizona* 8 x 10 (see Fig. 41)

Serene mtn. view from high on another mtn. Shadows, cast by high clouds, seem about to move. Deep, wide valley, curving Salt River. Twisted tree r. fgrd. Giant cacti and others. Delicately rendered in shades of gray; strong drypoint in fgrd. Monogram & © r.

269 *Evening, Painted Desert, Arizona* 5 x 7

A threatening sky full of dark lines and white cumulus clouds. Tree with white, twisted trunk and dark clumps of leaves growing among rocks r. fgrd. Desert in middle distance. Pointed spine of mtn. ctr. distance. Angular, block-like mtns. to l. Monogram & © r. Cf. #256 *Arizona Storm*; #258 *Storm in the Painted Desert, Arizona*; #260 *Storm on the Little Colorado River, Arizona*.

270   *First Snow* [no. 2]   3½ x 3½
Twisted trees and shrubs. Snow mostly on ground. Dark, icy stream ctr. fgrd.
to r. corner is shaped like back of r. hand with fingers curled under, wrist to
low r. of ctr. Stream is black, lowest part executed in vertical and horizontal
lines; no reflections. Etched lines in sky. Monogram l. Cf. #61 *First Snow* [no. 1];
also #151 *Snow,* in which stream has similar shape.

271   *Oaks in Winter* [no. 2]   9 x 7
This is #81 *Oaks in Winter* [no. 1] reworked. Plate cut 1″ shorter, monogram
placed on r. [My copy: title on lower l. edge of lower margin, not in Burr's
handwriting.]

272   *Pyramid Mountain, New Mexico*   2⅝ x 4⅝
Profile of large, dark, pyramid-shaped mtn. of solid rock resting on a base
of straight-sided rock. Highest point in ctr. In fgrd. r. a horse and rider. Sagebrush. Monogram l. [Pyramid Rock, of red sandstone, is near Gallup, just west
of Church Rock (see #210 *Navajo Church, New Mexico*).]

273   *Brook in Winter No. 3*   10 x 8
Large snow-spotted tree l. fgrd., other trees in middle ground, small trees beyond.
Intricate patterns of many leafless branches all snow-laden. Snow came from l.,
sticking to l. side of tree trunks. Many vertical lines mirror straight trunks in icy
stream ctr. to r. corner. Dark sky. Strong contrasts. Cold and dampness clearly
portrayed. Monogram l. Cf. #297 *Woods in Winter,* same size.

274   *Evening, Apache Trail, Arizona*   5 x 7   (see Fig. 42)
On l. an ancient, twisted, windblown tree with large trunk, some bare branches,
some leaved. On r. a deep chasm with rocky cliffs, eroded mtns. etched in fine,
delicate lines. Monogram & © l. Sometimes confused with #299 *Hassayampa
River, Arizona* (q.v.). [My copy: rice paper.]

275   *Canyon Rim, Arizona*   10 x 8
Weatherbeaten trees in a cluster l. with tenacious foothold among fissures in
steep cliffs and precipitously slanted rocks. Ctr. and r., a view down into the
Grand Canyon. Colorado River dimly seen in lower r. Shadows on canyon walls
lower r. in shape of letter *J.* Round clouds. Monogram l. This, the second of three
plates of the same subject, might well have been titled *Grand Canyon No. 2.*
Cf. #330 *Grand Canyon Plate 3.* See also #212 *Grand Canyon* [no. 1] in the
Desert Set.

276   *Misty Day, Pauls Wharf, London*   10 x 8   (see Fig. 43)
In fgrd., dark barges with steersmen in stern. Strong, dark reflections. In middle
distance, other craft. Many buildings in shades of gray lining opposite bank
of river. "PAULS WHARF" high on each of two buildings ctr. and l. Above all
rises stately dome of St. Paul's, its clock tower to l. Gentle rain and mist. Monogram l. [Although St. Paul's Cathedral was spared, this district along the Thames
was badly damaged in World War II.]

277   *Coast at Monterey, California*   10 x 8   (see Fig. 44)
A few venerable, weatherbeaten trees growing on rocky promontory fill entire l.
Pacific Ocean low r., round, billowing clouds, interesting sky, rain streaks. Con-

George Elbert Burr   *Desert Wrens, nest*

Figure 47 — #290 *Nest of the Desert Wren, Arizona*   8 x 5 inches

trast of light and dark. Monogram l. See #235 *Old Cypress near Monterey*, similar subject, different size. [My copy: no signature; no title.]

278   *Eucalyptus Trees, Santa Barbara*   10 x 7
Two tall, slender, delicate trees with white, dappled trunks r. of ctr. All shadows at their bases and in fgrd. are from l. and form right angles with straight tree trunks. Other trees and house form interesting and varied bgrd. Pale new moon in upper l. quadrant. Monogram l.

279   *Old Charcoal Boat, Venice* [no. 3]   5 x 8
Cargo boat, arched cover over hold, tillerman seated high in stern between double rudders, trapezium sail aft, a second man amidships plying long oar. A similar boat with sail closer to shore. Other sailing craft l. distance, small craft dockside r. Sketchy buildings. Reflections in water. Fades to edges. Monogram r. This is an etching; its description applies also to #352 *Charcoal Boat, Venice* [no. 2], executed in drypoint. I have not seen #79 *Charcoal Boat, Venice* [no. 1], same size.

280   *Misty Moonlight, Estes Park, Colorado*   10 x 7
This is #164 *In Estes Park* [no. 1] (q.v.) reworked. Night scene; full moon ctr. is shining on snow-covered Longs Peak l., and aquatint is added to give misty effect in dark sky, otherwise description is the same. Monogram r.

281   *Whirlwinds, Dead Mountains, Mojave Desert, California* [no. 2]
   8 x 10
Large, dark, sharply pointed mtn. in middle distance r., others l. and beyond in far distance. Two whirlwinds l. of ctr. in middle distance casting long shadows to r. on white sand. Suggestion of a third far l. in distance. Two large, dark clumps of vegetation near lower l. corner amidst a scattered group of flora dwindling to r. and disappearing about 1″ from r. edge. Delicate and hauntingly beautiful. Monogram l. Cf. #197 *Whirlwinds, Mojave Desert* [no. 1] and #312 *Whirlwinds* [no. 3].

282   *Evening, Paradise Valley, Arizona*   8 x 10   (see Fig. 45)
Beautiful, restful desert landscape. Clouds in small cottony puffs and streaks hover over sharp-pointed dark mtns. that form bgrd. for lush growth of desert flora. Giant cacti, two close together l. fgrd. partially silhouetted against sky. Thick growth of ocotillo, cholla, barrel cactus, etc. on valley floor. Large, dark cloud shadows through ctr., small shadows beneath flora to r. Monogram r. Similar to #319 *Paradise Valley, Arizona* (q.v.). [Paradise Valley, near Phoenix and just beyond Camelback Mountain, has now lost something of its pristine charm.]

283   *Springtime, Paradise Valley, Arizona*   12 x 10
Pleasant desert landscape. Three tall yuccas (Spanish bayonet) with many blooms in exquisite detail. Others in bgrd. Many varieties of cactus, mostly low-growing. Shadow and sunlight. Mtn. horizon lowest one-fifth of plate. Streaks in sky from upper l. Monogram r.

284   *The Edge of the Desert, Arizona*   10 x 12
Thickly tangled trees in fgrd. upper l. down toward r. corner, framing and screening view of white desert far below and buttes beyond. Rocky cliffs in sunlight rise high r. of ctr. Billowing clouds near horizon. Angry sky above. Rainbow arc high in sky. Many lines. Monogram l.

285   *On Lake Lugano, Italy* [no. 2]   10 x 7
This is #231 *Village Street, Lake Lugano, Italy* [no. 1] (q.v.), plate cut on all four sides and reworked. Many shading lines added in several areas. No date on plate. Monogram r. Cf. #349 *Lake Lugano, Italy* [no. 3].

286   *Soapweed, Arizona* [no. 2]   10 x 7   (see Fig. 46)
Against a dark sky, five spikes of waxy-white blossoms in exquisite detail, and dark, sharp-pointed leaves, all in ctr. to l. Desert flora fgrd. to r. distance. Tall saguaro cactus, ocotillo, mtn. skyline, and cumulus clouds add interest to r. Monogram r. Cf. #191 *Soapweed* [no. 1] in the Desert Set.

287   *A Mirage, Arizona* [no. 2]   8 x 10
Profusion of desert flora in fgrd. strongly contrasting with rest of landscape. Bgrd. of sharp-pointed mtns. In middle distance a beautiful mirage of lake reflects pale, eroded mtns. r. and l. Monogram l. Not to be confused with #194 *A Mirage* [no. 1] (q.v.) in the Desert Set.

288   *Barrel Cactus* [no. 2]   7 x 5
A spiny barrel cactus crowned by its blossoms, shown in painstaking detail. Terrain slopes gently from l. down to r. Pointed mtns. on horizon. Monogram l. Easily confused with #205 *Barrel Cactus* [no. 1] (q.v.) in the Desert Set.

289   *Ocotillo, Arizona* [no. 2]   8 x 5
Desert mtns. and desert floor seen through spreading, thorny stems of two ocotillos, clusters of blossoms on tips. Other flora interest. Cloudless. Monogram r. [My copy: no title.]

290   *Nest of the Desert Wren, Arizona*   8 x 5   (see Fig. 47)
Cholla cactus depicted in scrupulous detail. A bird standing on top l., its nest below. Fgrd. littered with small, spiny joints that have fallen from cactus. Decorative interest. Sky crosshatched. Monogram l.

291   *"Cucumber" Cactus, Arizona*   7 x 5
Many stems of low-growing hedgehog cactus r. of ctr. with large blossoms on ends, apparently rising from a central root system. Heavy shadows to r. At l. a feathery, graceful creosote (greasewood) bush affords contrast. Irregular skyline. Monogram l. [The stems of this cactus, which seldom attains a height of more than one foot, sometimes resemble spiny cucumbers.]

292   *Indian Home, Salt River Mountains, Arizona*   8 x 10
Small house r. with long roof extended toward l., making shade for seated figure. Live tree far r. Pottery jars. Giant cacti ctr., bushes, abundant and varied flora l. to middle distance. Dark mtn. r. behind house. Large mtn. in bgrd. to l. margin. White clouds r. of ctr. casting shadows on mtns. Monogram r. Cf. #294 *Indian Homes, Apache Reservation, Arizona.*

293   *Evening, Navajo Country, Arizona*   10 x 12
Luminous cloud in dark sky. Mesa ctr. distance still plainly seen in reflected light. Others l. and r. Large flock of sheep ctr. fgrd., shepherd and dog r. seen in half-light. Tree l. corner. Monogram r. [Edition estimated at 150. Burr wrote to R. P. Tolman (Oct. 14, 1929) that this etching "is intended to be a poem of twilight, in the great open desert, and, like a fine poem, doesn't give all to one

at once. . . . I played with this plate for a year, and put in it all I know as to a tonal *finished* plate. . . . The plate is dry point, but as I worked I cut off the burr, and went over it again and again like one can do with a pencil, 'til lines disappear. The little bit of softness in the light is done by pressing sand paper on the copper and making little catches of roughness, this to avoid making the plate look overworked.

"The work was *all* a delicate job — so delicate, I had the plate steeled so that I have a hundred prints all alike in quality. The plate wouldn't have made more than fifteen otherwise."]

294 *Indian Homes, Apache Reservation, Arizona* 8 x 10 (see Fig. 48)
Two figures seated under thatched shelter held up by poles and nestled against a thick shrub l. of ctr. In ctr. a small covered haystack, a ladder and pieces of wood leaning against it, other pieces on ground. To r. two branch-covered huts, one with small door, dead tree rising tall above and behind them. Small live tree in l. fgrd. No clouds. Monogram l. Cf. #292 *Indian Home, Salt River Mountains, Arizona.*

295 *Road to Apache Reservation, Arizona* 10 x 8
Many giant cacti, tops silhouetted against cloudless sky. Horse with rider wearing a brimmed hat, approaching on curving road in r. corner. Many bushes and plants. Ground rises slightly from fgrd. Short shadows to l. Monogram l.

296 *In Estes Park, Colorado* [no. 2] 10 x 8
Two imperfectly shaped trees standing together l. of ctr. above tree-clad mtn. slope. Smaller one on l. has split trunk; larger one has curved trunk. Underneath long, low branch flung out to r. a view of mtns. and park with snow-clad Longs Peak in far distance. Monogram l.

297 *Woods in Winter* 10 x 8
On farther bank of icy stream, trees of all sizes, a tangled mass of leafless branches, twigs, etc. Narrow icy stream from below ctr. l. to r. corner. Ground lightly covered with snow, trees only spotted. Ground rises to r. Monogram r. Cf. #273 *Brook in Winter No. 3.*

298 *Sketch on Apache Trail, Arizona* 7 x 5
Pale, eroded, rocky cliffs form bgrd. with dark canyon r. of ctr. Weatherbeaten tree lower r. corner, two saguaro cacti l. corner, twisting Salt River in valley ctr. Dark, rocky cliffs on l. Forbidding but attractive. Monogram r. Easily confused with #264 *Fish Creek, Apache Trail, Arizona* (q.v.). [My copy: title on lower edge of lower margin, not in Burr's handwriting.]

299 *Hassayampa River, Arizona* 5 x 7
Ancient, curiously misshapen cedar tree occupies fgrd. l., its branches windblown mostly to r. Beneath them in far r. distance a river-bend with a few rounded trees along its banks, and a flat valley. No clouds. Monogram l. On margins of some copies Burr penciled a version of the Hassayampa Legend. On copies in Boston Museum of Fine Arts and Denver Public Library:

> If you drink its water,
> You will never tell the truth,
> Own a dollar, or leave Arizona.

Sometimes confused with #274 *Evening, Apache Trail, Arizona* (q.v.). [The

Hassayampa flows south from near Prescott, joining the Gila River west of Phoenix.]

300 *The Etcher* 7 x 5 (see Frontispiece)
Self-portrait, three-quarter length. Profile of man facing r., examining etching plate held in hands. Glasses, shirt with white collar and sleeves rolled to elbows, dark bib apron. At r., wheel and rollers of geared press. Majority of lines in this etching are vertical. Bgrd. darkest directly behind figure. Monogram r.

301 *Twilight, New Mexico* [no. 3] 5 x 7*
Have not found this etching.

302 *Youth and Age* 10 x 8*
Have not found this etching.

303 *Arizona Sunshine* [nude] 10 x 8
Straight front view of nude standing, hands on hips, arms akimbo. Heavy face. Bgrd. of mtns., desert flora, wide valley. Monogram l.

304 *Palo Verde* [nude] 5 x 7
Palo verde tree furnishes dark bgrd. for nude lying on back; head, at l., turned to face viewer. R. leg drawn up. Monogram r.

305 *Desert Poppies* [nude] 5 x 7
Poppies in bloom and sharp distant mtns. are bgrd. for reclining nude with head at r. slightly raised, hands behind head. Monogram r.

306 *Sand Dunes* [nude] 6 x 8; 4¾ x 6¾
Suggestion of sand dunes forms bgrd. for nude sitting on ground, one leg under her, balancing weight on r. hand, r. arm straight, l. arm hanging. Heavy face. Monogram r.

307 *New Moon* [nude] 5 x 7
New moon upper l. Nude lying on sand, dark hair streaming, l. hand on body, r. hand on sand. Monogram r.

308 *Yuccas* [nude] 8 x 10
Two desert yuccas l. and mtns. form bgrd. for nude resting on l. arm, r. hand holding dark tresses, l. leg bent at knee and l. foot under r. leg. Monogram r.

309 *Apache Maid* [nude] 8 x 10
Dark-skinned nude, dark hair parted in ctr. and falling past shoulders, standing with arms crossed, covering breasts. Detailed face. Monogram l. [The other sketches of nudes in this group are titled according to bgrd.]

310 *Old Cedar* [nude] 8 x 10
Nude sitting on ancient cedar tree, hands behind head, feet on roots, facing three-quarters l. Monogram r. Tree similar to that in #317 *Old Cedar, Ash Fork, Arizona* (q.v.).

311   *Dawn* [nude]   10 x 8
Step-like rock formations r., buttes and mtns. ctr. distance form bgrd. Nude standing ctr., both hands raising strands of her dark hair high above head. Monogram l.

312   *Whirlwinds* [no. 3]   8 x 10
Dark, sharp-pointed peaks in bgrd., highest l. of ctr. Three delicately portrayed whirlwinds, two in middle distance l. of ctr., one far r. distance. Shadows to r. Scattered round, black creosote bushes on white sand entire l. to r. arranged in lines. Bushes in fgrd. in heavy drypoint. Monogram r. Probably same locale in southern California as #197 *Whirlwinds, Mojave Desert* [no. 1] in the Desert Set, and #281 *Whirlwinds, Dead Mountains, Mojave Desert, California* [no. 2] (q.v.).

313   *Solitude*   8 x 10*
Have not found this etching.

314   *Arizona Night*   8 x 10   (see Fig. 49)
Dark, eerie landscape with many jagged mtn. peaks forming bgrd. entire l. to r. Full moon upper r. quadrant shining on several flat mountaintops in middle distance and l. to r. Single, indistinct tree lower l. corner, other vegetation spreading to r. and gently climbing on mtn. scree r. to corner. Vegetation visible in distant valley ctr. r. Monogram l. Somewhat similar to #187 *Desert Night* (q.v.) in the Desert Set.

315   *Near Needles, Arizona*   8 x 10; 7 x 9
Night scene with full moon upper l. Dark, jagged mtns. rising above sand r. middle distance. Three giant cacti, one palo verde tree, many small, scattered, round growths of desert flora. Pointed mtns. l. and r. far distance. Monogram l. Black ink with greenish tint sometimes used. [Burr's note on NYPL copy: "Private plate (American Etchers)" (i.e., Society of American Etchers, formerly Brooklyn Society of Etchers). See #367 *Evening, Arizona*, also privately printed for the same society.]

316   *Valley of the Lledr, Wales* [no. 2]   5 x 8
This is #92 *Valley of the Lledr, North Wales* [no. 1] reworked. Lines have been softened. Same description. Monogram r.

317   *Old Cedar, Ash Fork, Arizona*   10 x 12
Ghoulish figure of distorted tree growing out of rocks r. of ctr., its roots grasping for holds l. Thick trunk, many short and leaved branches. Glimpse of verdant valley l. with mtn. peaks in distance. Monogram r. Cf. #218 *Old Cedars, New Mexico* in the Desert Set. Tree similar to that in #310 *Old Cedar.*

318   *Desert Twilight*   5 x 6¾
Large white cloud r. of ctr., top almost pointed. Two small puffs of high clouds l. of ctr., other sharp-domed clouds far l. and r. Flat-topped mtns. ctr. to r., also middle distance l. Pointed mtns. on horizon l. of ctr. Dark fgrd. with a few trees r. Monogram r. Cf. #203 *Twilight, Laguna, New Mexico* [no. 2] in the Desert Set. [My copy: greenish dark-blue ink, a true color that I have seen before daybreak on the desert following a dust storm the evening before.]

George Elbert Burr.   Indian Homes – Apache Reservation Arizona

Figure 48 — #294 *Indian Homes, Apache Reservation, Arizona*   8 x 10 inches

319   *Paradise Valley, Arizona*   5 x 8

Several giant cacti, one with a single arm extreme r., ocotillos, one extreme l. near border, other desert flora standing on flat desert. Almost lush but not crowded. White clouds like cotton balls rising ctr. to r. Inconspicuous mtns. on low, far horizon. Small shadows to l. Painstakingly detailed. Monogram r. Similar to #282 *Evening, Paradise Valley, Arizona* (q.v.) and smaller.

320   *Mesa Encantada, New Mexico* [no. 2]   4¾ x 8

Famous mesa standing alone in flat desert, rain streaks and soft clouds beyond l. to r. Horizon interest. Strong shadings. Dark drypoint lines in fgrd. Monogram l. Sometimes confused with #216 *Mesa Encantada, New Mexico* [no. 1] (q.v.) in the Desert Set. [The Enchanted Mesa is a few miles south of Laguna.]

321   *Palm Canyon near Palm Springs* [no. 3]   7 x 5

Zigzag stream from ctr. fgrd. to ctr. middle distance, tall palm trees on high bank filling r. half of etching. Large group of palms of various sizes l. on farther bank. San Jacinto Mountains dimly seen in distance. Monogram l.

322   *Verde River, Apache Reservation, Arizona*   8 x 10

Peaceful landscape. One lone, shaft-like giant cactus with two stubby arms fgrd. Cacti, thick tangle of trees and bushes to l. and in middle distance. Flat river valley r. with light reflecting on water. Mtns. in bgrd. Cloud-filled sky. Monogram r.

323   *Dunes near Palm Springs, California* [no. 2]   5 x 7   (see Fig. 50)

Mtns. in shades of gray form entire bgrd. beyond soft-looking undulating sand dunes in middle distance and fgrd. A number of trees and bushes in lower l. corner. Pale shadows toward l. A study in delicate shadings. Monogram l. Easily confused with #199 *Desert Dunes* [no. 1] in the Desert Set. [My copy: no title.]

324   *The Land of Mystery — The Desert*   7 x 9½

Dark points of mtns. rise from a sea of sand. Two riders and three pack animals l. heading r. Streaks of scrubby bushes in vast white, sandy desert. A few puffs of clouds r. Two birds in flight l. Monogram r.

325   *Superstition Mountain, Apache Trail, Arizona, Night* [no. 2]
        12 x 10   (see Fig. 51)

A remarkably tranquil scene: massive, luminous cloud in dark sky; pale light striking large, angular mtn., stately and brooding. Fgrd. dark; giant cacti and other vegetation dimly seen. Monogram l. See #250 *Superstition Mountain, Apache Trail, Arizona* [no. 1]. [For honors accorded this etching, see Chapter II under years 1931–32.]

326   *Winter No. 2*   7 x 10   (see Fig. 52)

This is #62 *Winter* [no. 1], plate reworked. Same general description but clearer, more fine-lined details; contrast of shadings more definite; shadows and reflections in stream more pronounced. Monogram r. [My duplicate copy: *Winter*, without number.]

327   *Road to Bear Lake*   10 x 8   (see Fig. 53)

Hallett Peak in ctr. distance with snow in crevices and wide patch of snow r., framed by dark and interesting trees in fgrd., some with bare tops and dead branches, some fallen, all suggesting proximity of timber line. Mtn. stream and bushes in immediate fgrd. Monogram l. See #328 *Longs Peak, Estes Park, Colorado* [no. 4]. [Both subjects are in Rocky Mountain National Park.]

328   *Longs Peak, Estes Park, Colorado* [no. 4]   9¾ x 7¾   (see Fig. 54)
Dark trees with foliage completely frame Longs Peak on r. and Mt. Meeker on l., both pale and snowy in distance. Sunlight on park in middle distance, dark foothills just beyond. A patch of sunlight on rocky mtn. slope surrounded by trees. Restful, inviting spot. Monogram r. See #327 *Road to Bear Lake*, similar in subject matter, treatment, and mood; together they make a harmonious pair. Burr made a lithograph, 10 x 13⅞, with same title.

329   *New Moon and Morning Star, Phoenix, Arizona*   10 x 8
New moon and bright star upper r. quadrant above jagged mtns. In l. fgrd. a beautiful specimen of tall, many-branched saguaro cactus, three others l. and r. Uncrowded spots of vegetation. Enthralling night scene. Monogram r.

330   *Grand Canyon Plate 3*   10 x 8
Composition similar to #275 *Canyon Rim, Arizona* (q.v.). Two straight trees l. fgrd., their leaved or bare branches extending to top and sides of etching. Gradual and delicate shadings of walls and eroded peaks. Two canyon peaks in distance r. Light reflects on Colorado River in lower r. Monogram l. See also #212 *Grand Canyon* [no. 1], a dramatic soft ground in the Desert Set.

331   *Palm Canyon Plate 2*   10 x 8
A line-for-line enlargement of #192 *Palm Canyon* [no. 1] in the Desert Set. Monogram l. [My copy: *Palm Canyon, Calif.* on lower l. edge of bottom margin, not in Burr's handwriting.]

332   *Spanish Peaks, Colorado* [no. 3]   8 x 10
In r. fgrd. two tall, straight trees standing in front of rounded trees. Mesas in l. middle distance. The two Spanish Peaks in far distance l., snow on summits. No clouds. Strong contrast between drypoint and white areas. Bare and uncluttered. Monogram l.

333   *Desert Clouds*   11¾ x 10
Black trees with white trunks leaning gracefully on terrain that slopes from l. fgrd. toward r. corner, affording a glimpse of distant valley and pointed mtn. Build-up of white mass of cottony clouds somewhat repeats black areas of the tree leaves. Monogram l. upside down. Cf. #217 *Piñon Trees*. Burr made a lithograph, *Desert Cloud*, 14 x 11¾.

334   *Evening on the Little Colorado River*   10 x 12
Three trees with white trunks r. of ctr., dark leaves, branches swept l., strong shadows to l. Sharp-leaved grasses. In distance far l. a mtn. with horizontal strata. Top of mtn. l. below ctr. Horizontal streaks of clouds. L. of ctr. large white cloud, others l. and r. Monogram l. Not to be confused with #265 *Summer Cloud, Apache Trail, Arizona.*

335   *Desert Monuments, Arizona*   10 x 12   (see Fig. 55)
Ancient, eroded buttes in fine-lined detail, standing on vast desert. Two riders and one pack animal r. of ctr. heading l. Spotty and scattered sagebrush. Monogram r. [Locale: Monument Valley, in Navajo County near Utah border.]

336 *San Gorgonio from the Coachella Valley, California* 8 x 10
Two palm trees r. of ctr. and a horse and rider l. of ctr. focus view on vast valley in middle distance and on snow-capped San Gorgonio in far distance ctr. Other, darker mtns. l. and r. Monogram l. [Locale: near Palm Springs.]

337 *Painted Cliffs, Apache Trail, Arizona* 10 x 8
Steep cliffs descending sharply from upper l. to r. of ctr., heavily inked, partially frame view of sunlit desert mtns. rising from Salt River Canyon. Giant cacti and others, and several bushy trees middle distance. Sunshine and shade. Sketchy clouds r. Monogram l.

338 *Mountain of the Holy Cross* 10 x 8
Dark, massive mtn., viewed from near timber line, rises to summit top ctr. On its rocky and barren side, snow-filled fissures form a cross. Smaller streaks of snow on either side. Straight, tall tree r. fgrd., cutting about one-fifth of plate top to bottom, frames focal point with other trees l. Fgrd. entirely rocks. Serene view. Monogram l. [Vantage points for viewing this landmark are far more accessible today than when Burr was roaming these mtns., often at altitudes of 10,000 feet and higher, over a period of nearly twenty years prior to 1924. Although the Mountain of the Holy Cross is no longer a National Monument owing to disfiguring rock slides and erosion, the long fissure (1,500 feet) and one arm (750 feet) have not been affected. Locale: Sawatch Range, White River National Forest.]

339 *San Francisco Peaks, Arizona* [no. 2] 8 x 10
Massive, solid, impressive mtns. entire bgrd. l. to r. Clouds above make shadows on mtns. and desert-like floor. Dark trees l. fgrd. Numerous trees scattered l. to r. in middle distance. Monogram l. Cf. #222 *San Francisco Mountains, Arizona* [no. 1] in the Desert Set, slightly smaller.

340 *Sketch in Taormina, Sicily* 12 x 10
Village street ctr. leading to stucco house with tile roof, arched doorway, two seated figures, clothes on line l. Large, graceful olive tree l. fgrd. Plain, high wall of house r. fgrd. In bgrd., mtn. with ancient fortress-castle perched on top. Fades toward edges. Monogram l. [Burr's note on NYPL copy: "Six proofs, plate destroyed."]

341 *Chimney Pots, Lausanne, Suisse* (No measurements available)
Have not found this etching.

342 *Old House in Wye Valley* 8 x 10
House in Wales; thatched roof, bottom line broken by two windows. Extensions of house to l. and r. have tile roof. Large chimney r., trees l. Stone fence with two gates. Sketchy. Monogram l. [Burr's note on NYPL copy: "12 proofs, plate destroyed."]

343 *Harlech Castle, Wales* 8 x 9¾
Fortress-castle seen from same elevation, showing its distinctive, nearly square plan, thick, straight walls, and round towers at corners. Houses and trees in l. fgrd. Flat land (covered by the sea 600 years ago) below on r. A few houses. Straight roads. Mtns. of Snowdonia form bgrd. Monogram l. of ctr. [Well-preserved ruins of thirteenth-century castle built on high vantage point over-

146

George Elbert Burr

Arizona Night

Figure 49 — #314 *Arizona Night*   8 x 10 inches

looking Tremadoc Bay (at north end of Cardigan Bay) on coast of North Wales. Burr's note on NYPL copy: "Eight proofs, plate destroyed."]

344 *Oberlahnstein, Rhine* 8 x 10
Martinsburg Castle, octagonal tower on l. and taller, square tower with pointed roof on r. Suggestion of mtn. r. distance. Low wall in fgrd., female figure approaching gate. Sketchy. Fades to edges. Monogram ctr. [This rather small castle, dating from fourteenth century and still occupied, is located in town of Oberlahnstein on r. bank of the Rhine, just above its juncture with the Lahn. Exterior lines not much changed since Burr was there. My copy: No. 4/10; "Ten proofs — plate destroyed."]

345 *Sketch of Florence from San Miniato* [no. 3] 8 x 9¾
Panoramic view of Florence. Reverse or offset print: in this version tower of Palazzo Vecchio is on l. Shops on middle of three bridges. Monogram r. Cf. #54 *Florence from San Miniato* [no. 1] and #67 *Florence from San Miniato* [no. 2]. [Burr's note on NYPL copy: "Four proofs, plate destroyed."]

346 *Florence from Monte Oliveto* [no. 3] 7 x 9
Reverse print. See #39 *Florence from Monte Oliveto* [no. 1], in color, and #242 *Florence from Monte Oliveto* [no. 2]. In this, a less dramatic version, the trees are smaller, largest olive tree is on r. Sketchy. Monogram r. [Burr's note on NYPL copy: "Eight proofs, plate destroyed."]

347 *Valley at Toblach, Tyrol* 7 x 9
An inviting, rather narrow, fertile valley ctr. becomes tightly enclosed by sharply ascending mtns., partially tree-clad but barren at their peaks. Monogram r. [Town and valley, near Brenner Pass, are known locally by both their Austrian and Italian names: Toblach and Pustertal, or Dobbiaco and Val Pusteria. Burr's note on NYPL copy: "Six proofs, plate destroyed."]

348 *West Gate, Warwick* 9 x 7
Figures both in and outside of dark, arched doorway in massive tower with crenelated top, part of ancient city wall. Above, arched window of chapel, clock mounted in diamond-shaped frame. Generally sketchy effect. Title etched on plate l. of ctr. Monogram r. [Burr's note on NYPL copy: "Six proofs, plate destroyed."]

349 *Lake Lugano, Italy* [no. 3] 10 x 7¼
Similar to #231 *Village Street, Lake Lugano, Italy* [no. 1] and #285 *On Lake Lugano, Italy* [no. 2] (q.v.). Rectangular door, closed; oval window above. Cobbled street from door to lowest fgrd. r. of ctr. Street descends ctr. past wall and tile-roofed house with grapevine l. toward lake and mtns. seen through archway. Many lines. Spaces filled. Dark. Monogram l. of ctr. [Lake Lugano has shores in both Italy and Switzerland. Burr's note on NYPL copy: "Ten prints, plate destroyed."]

350 *Stone Pines near Sorrento, Italy* 12 x 10
Three tall pines, tallest on r. Olive trees fgrd. Isle of Capri across water in distance. Misty. No moon. Monogram l. Cf. #245 *Capri from Sorrento*. [Arizona State University copy: "Nine proofs, plate destroyed."]

351   *Iffley Mill near Oxford*   10½ x 12¼
Famous mill among trees l. of ctr., water wheel ctr. and a millrace. Tall, straight poplars r., and many other trees r. and l. All fgrd. is pond with little ripples and reflections; water pouring over dam ctr. fgrd. Monogram r. [My copy: "Eight proofs, plate destroyed."]

352   *Charcoal Boat, Venice* [no. 2]   5 x 8
This is a drypoint. Same description and size as #279 *Old Charcoal Boat, Venice* [no. 3], an etching. Monogram r. I have not seen #79 *Charcoal Boat, Venice* [no. 1], same size.

353   *Old Bridge, Chester, England* [no. 2]   5 x 8
A drypoint and soft ground made from same sketch as #88 *Old Bridge, Chester* [no. 1], an etching. Sketchy effect, no clouds, no fisherman, otherwise same description. Monogram l. [See #52 *Heidelberg, Sunset* and footnote listing other bridges. My copy: "Five proofs, plate destroyed."]

354   *Valley of the Llugwy, Wales*   5 x 8
River lower l. flowing into distance, rounded trees on its banks. Suggested mtn. skyline (Moelwyn Siabod Range). Sketchy. Monogram r. Cf. #94 *Moel Siabod, North Wales*. [My copy: trial proof; "Four proofs — plate destroyed."]

355   *Devil's Bridge near Lucca, Italy* (No measurements available)
Have not found this etching. [Located at Bagni di Lucca in northern Italy, the Ponte del Diavolo is fourteenth-century stone bridge over the Serchio River. It is high and narrow, and bends slightly; largest and highest arch is in ctr. Mtns. form bgrd. on all sides. See #52 *Heidelberg, Sunset* and footnote listing other bridges.]

356   *Old Cedar near Kingman, Arizona*   9½ x 7⅞   (see Fig. 56)
Ancient, bent, and twisted old cedar in fgrd., its thick trunk on r. curved l.; many leaves in ctr., dead branches raised toward upper l. Tree leaning as if about to fall. Full moon l., seen from under lowest branches, is dimly shining on strange, flat mtns. Unreal, dreamlike. Monogram r. [Nos. 315–356 are recorded on two sheets of notebook paper in Burr's holograph list in NYPL. If #356 can be considered his last etching made for general sale, and if, as has often been suggested, his trees sometimes bear resemblance to humans, then this etching might be regarded as a kind of frank and revealing self-portait of the artist made around 1935, in his 76th year. My copy: no title.]

357   *Low Tide, North Wales* [no. 2]   8 x 9¾
Probably made from same sketch #87 *Low Tide, North Wales* [no. 1] (q.v.). Has unfinished appearance. Monogram r. [Burr's note on NYPL copy: "Four proofs, plate destroyed."]

358   *[Examples of Intaglio Processes]*   2⅞ x 7
On one plate, eight examples of etcher's techniques, each labeled by Burr: mezzotint (rectangle); drypoint (nude); sandpaper tint (square); engraved lines (group of lines); aquatint (landscape with mtns., moon, sky); soft ground (tree); etching (castle); roulette tint (lines and shading).

359 *Sketch in the Mojave Desert* 3¼ x 6⅞
Buttes l. and r. in drypoint. Black lines and shadows l. to r. fgrd., pale mtns. in distance l. to r. Monogram l. [Burr's note on NYPL copy: "Plate never finished."]

360 *Brook and Trees, Winter* 6 x 3½
Brook ctr. to lower l., tall tree on r. leans r. Old forked tree l. of stream. Others, all snowy. Many small black dots on tree trunk and bushes in fgrd. No monogram. [Burr's note on NYPL copy: "Plate never finished or printed."]

361 *Portrait of the Artist* 6 x 4
Bust, front view; eyeglasses, hair parted in middle. Monogram l. upside down. [This may have been made from a studio photograph (one in my collection, another in the Fogg Art Museum) that appears, cropped, as frontispiece in Lena McCauley's pamphlet *George Elbert Burr, Painter-Etcher* (1923). Burr's note on NYPL copy: "One proof only, plate destroyed 10/24/29."]

362 *Indian Homes, Colorado River, Arizona* 7½ x 11¾
Three Indian homes close together, two seated figures in shade under extended roof. River in middle distance l. Mtns. form bgrd. No clouds. Monogram & © l. [Burr's note on NYPL copy: "Three proofs, plate destroyed."]

363 *Near Our Cabin* 5 x 8
Pyramidal mtn., its peak high and r. of ctr. Dark rocks, scrubby bushes to r. A mtn. slope with trees on ridge descends past ctr.; another slope just beyond. Expanse of plains l., mesas beyond. Clouds ctr. Monogram r. [Burr's note on NYPL copy: "Four proofs, plate destroyed, unfinished."]

364 *[My First Etching]* 3 x 4½
Fallen horizontal logs, ferns in fgrd. Dark shadows in ctr. Inferior paper. [Burr's note on NYPL copy: "My first etching made on thin scrap of 'Tin Shop' copper, and printed by rolling between steel bending rollers in 'Tin Shop' about 1872. George Elbert Burr." This and #365 were made when the artist was between twelve and fifteen years of age, in the tin shop that was part of his father's store in Cameron, Missouri.]

365 *[My Second Attempt at Etching]* 4½ x 3
Tree with large trunk, leaning from lower l. to upper r. and filling most of area. Shading on r. side. "BURR" lower l. on plate. Some fgrd. interest. [Burr's note on NYPL copy: "My second attempt at etching. Made on scrap tinshop copper and printed by running between steel rollers in tin shop, 1874. G.E.B." See last remark under #364.]

366 *[Cactus Club Dinner Etching]* 5½ x 2½
Old pine tree ctr. standing among rocks, mountaintop in distance. On plate, "CACTUS CLUB MCH 1917." Lower l. in pencil: "G.E.B." Printed on upper half of card. [Burr was an honorary member. His note on NYPL copy: "Etched and printed at a dinner, Denver, Colo., March 1917. 3 Prints."]

367 *Evening, Arizona* 5 x 7
Desert landscape. Group of three dark yuccas (Spanish bayonet) in bloom r. of ctr., another farther r.; white, pointed mtns. directly behind them in middle distance. Dark, pointed mtns. l. of ctr. form bgrd. Dark sky, billowing clouds

George Elbert Burr

FIGURE 50 — #323 *Dunes near Palm Springs, California* [no. 2]   5 x 7 inches

rising high l. of ctr. Several varieties of cactus in sandy fgrd. Exquisitely delicate shadings. Monogram l. [John Taylor Arms in an open letter, 1930: "Plate etched especially for the Associate Members of the Brooklyn Society of Etchers. . . . Four hundred proofs were pulled and the plate destroyed." See #315 *Near Needles, Arizona,* also privately printed for the same society after its name was changed to Society of American Etchers. My copy: title lower l. edge of lower margin, not in Burr's handwriting.]

VII

Finding List of Burr Etchings Reproduced in Books, Periodicals, Newspapers, etc.

Table of Abbreviations. For book titles see Selected Bibliography.

Allhusen	E. L. Allhusen, *George Elbert Burr, Etcher*
AmEtchers	*George Elbert Burr.* American Etchers series
AmMArt	*American Magazine of Art*
AmPr	*American Prints in the Library of Congress*
ArizHi	*Arizona Highways*
Arizon	*The Arizonian* (Scottsdale, Ariz.)
ArizR	*Arizona Republic* (Phoenix)
ArtAm	*Art in America*
ArtD	*Art Digest*
ArtN	*Art News*
Arts&Dec	*Arts and Decoration*
ArtW	*Art World*
Atlan	*The Atlantic Monthly*
CalA&A	*California Arts & Architecture*
CDen	*City of Denver*
CrArt	*Creative Art*
DP	*Denver Post*
DT	*Denver Times*
FifPrYr	*Fifty Prints of the Year*
FPr	*Fine Prints*
FPrYr	*Fine Prints of the Year*
IntStud	*International Studio*
Laver	James Laver, *A History of British and American Etching*
McCauley	Lena M. McCauley, *George Elbert Burr's Etchings of the Desert*
MilwInstBul	*Bulletin of the Milwaukee Art Institute*

MinnInstBul	*Bulletin of the Minneapolis Institute of Arts*
Morse	A. Reynolds Morse, *George Elbert Burr*
MunF	*Municipal Facts* (Denver)
NYSun	*New York Sun*
NYT	*New York Times*
OkCT	*Oklahoma City Times*
100AmPr	*100 American Prints*
OpD	*Open Door* (Denver)
Outl	*The Outlook*
Pr	*Prints*
PrCollQ	*Print Collector's Quarterly*
PrConn	*Print Connoisseur*
RMN	*Rocky Mountain News* (Denver)
Roundup	*The Denver Westerners Monthly Roundup*
RVB	*Revue du vrai et du beau* (Paris)
Ss	*Sunset* (San Francisco)
Stud	*The Studio* (London)
Sun	*The Sun* (Flagstaff, Ariz.)
WashSt	*Washington* [D.C.] *Star*
WestDP	The Westerners, Denver Posse, *Brand Book*
YrbAmEtching	*Year Book of American Etching*

Locations. Before using this list, check for possible alternate titles in Chapter V.

254 *Arizona Canal, Phoenix*
Allhusen
Arizon, XV (Sept. 22, 1927)
PrConn, X (Oct. 1930)

184 *Arizona Clouds* [no. 2]
McCauley
WestDP, 1963

256 *Arizona Storm*
AmEtchers

205 *Barrel Cactus* [no. 1]
IntStud, LXXVIII (Oct. 1923)
McCauley

229 *Bear Creek Canyon, Denver, Colorado*
Allhusen
FPrYr, 1925
NYT, Jul. 17, 1927
PrConn, III (Apr. 1923)
RMN, Nov. 25, 1928

171 *Bent Pine, Estes Park*
DT, Mar. 30, 1916

175 *Black Canyon, Estes Park*
AmMArt, X (Feb. 1919)

273 *Brook in Winter No. 3*
Allhusen, under title *Brook in Winter (No. 2)*

161 *Brothers*
AmMArt, X (Feb. 1919)
Stud, II (Mar. 1928)

275 *Canyon Rim, Arizona*
Allhusen
AmEtchers
AmMArt, XX (June 1929)
ArizHi, XV (Aug. 1939)
ArtW, XIV (Dec. 24, 1929)
Atlan, CCXI (Mar. 1963)
PrConn, X (Oct. 1930), in two formats

79 *Charcoal Boat, Venice* [no. 1]
CDen, III (Nov. 28, 1914), under title *Venetian Charcoal Boat*
DP, Nov. 18, 1914

200 *Cholla Cactus*
McCauley
PrCollQ, XV (Oct. 1928)

FIGURE 51 — #325 *Superstition Mountain, Apache Trail, Arizona, Night* [no. 2]   12 x 10 inches

George Ebert Burr

Winter

Figure 52 — #326 *Winter No. 2*   7 x 10 inches

George Elbert Burr

On Road to Bear Lake. Estes Park. Colorado

Figure 53 — #327 *Road to Bear Lake*   10 x 8 inches

George Elbert Burr

Longs Peak - Estes Park - Colo-

FIGURE 54 — #328 *Longs Peak, Estes Park, Colorado* [no. 4]   9¾ x 7¾ inches

FIGURE 55 — #335 *Desert Monuments, Arizona*   10 x 12 inches

George Elbert Burr

FIGURE 56 — #356 *Old Cedar near Kingman, Arizona*   9½ x 7⅞ inches

FIGURE 57 — *Venice*   14 x 9¾ inches

This watercolor of Santa Maria della Salute, dated July 15, 1900, hung for some
thirty years in the Burr home

Appendix. Watercolors

IT HAS BEEN SHOWN in the course of Chapters I–III that during his early travels in Europe and subsequent residence in New Jersey Burr worked almost exclusively in watercolors, earning both his livelihood and a considerable reputation in that medium before moving to Denver in 1906. In the fall of that year he held a one-man show and was acclaimed by the *Denver Post* of October 21 as "one of America's leading water-color workers," a ranking consistent with the praise that his numerous exhibitions had earlier received in eastern cities. Until then he had for the most part painted European subjects, and in a manner that delighted the critics for reasons suggested by a review in the *Philadelphia Evening Telegraph* of his exhibit at Earle's Galleries in that city:

> He is one of the modern fraternity of outdoors painters, and his work has all the fresh, crisp quality of direct study from nature. [There is no] lack of the picturesque brilliance and tonal beauty only to be found in the finest watercolors. Mr. Burr has an appreciative sense of colors and a natural instinct for decorative effect. He sees rich color combinations where a less sensitive observer would only note low-keyed monotony, as for example in the group of old olive trees, gnarled, twisted, and ashen-grey, of which he makes most charming and delicate illustrations of the value of neutral tints. By contrast, some of his Italian and Alpine sunsets are made to shine like jewels; *Lake Geneva . . .* and *Sunset*

near Nevin [North Wales] . . . being examples of the splendid color qualities for which Turner's watercolors are so highly praised.[1]

The very next year Burr's second Denver show offered totally new subjects; the *Denver Post* of December 4, 1907, stated that it was "confined to California and Colorado views" and that Burr "finds more inspiration in the Rocky Mountains than in all the lofty ice-capped peaks of Switzerland. There is more color, more haze, more light and shadow. . . ." To portray faithfully the beauties of this rugged terrain, Burr continued his admirable, if strenuous, practice of painting in the open rather than in the studio from sketches. Two instances are recalled in the article cited. "Just before darkness settles over the little town at the mouth of Gore Cañon, there comes a blue glow that is seen nowhere outside of Kremmling in the entire state. Mr. Burr made his picture [*Evening Glow, Kremmling*], with the exception of the blue coloring, during the afternoon and painted the glow during the three to five minutes that it rested over the country. *In the Gore Cañon* is another picture that attracts not a little interest. In order to get into the cañon to study his subject, Mr. Burr went strapped to the sides of the rocks with the raging torrent below him."

Earlier, in 1905, when Burr was exhibiting thirty-nine watercolors at the Klackner Gallery in New York, the *New York Commercial Advertiser* remarked that he now and then broke away from his usual style, that he "disports himself with a visit into the land of sentiment and dreamy poetry, securing the mysteries of twilight, mist, or the early night, and in these he is generally successful, occasioning the wish that these journeys might be more frequent." Although they do not remind one of the calculated fantasy or the use of glowing color masses characteristic of the paintings of Maxfield Parrish, they doubtless would, indeed, have been well received during the era of his great popularity; but refreshing and (it can be presumed) somewhat experimental excursions such as *My Castle in Spain*[2] are not numerous among Burr's works, which, though decorative in their way, are not those of the illustrator, the poster artist, or the muralist.

His devotion to painting continued unabated through the twenties, by which time he was making an incredible number of etchings, and, in fact, it never waned; he estimated, as was mentioned in Chapter I, that he made more than a thousand watercolors. Most of these, except for subjects in which color played a predominant role (e.g., *A Santa*

[1] This and other press notices, all undated, were reprinted (probably by the Denver dealer Cyrus Boutwell, c. 1906) in a pamphlet that may be seen in the Denver Public Library, the Toledo Museum of Art (Stevens Collection), or on microfilm in the Archives of American Art, Detroit.

[2] This watercolor, done in 1920, is in the Denver Public Library. It is somewhat reminiscent of the *Youth* of Thomas Cole (d. 1848), in the Munson-Williams-Proctor Institute, Utica, N.Y. — one of his series *The Voyage of Life*.

Barbara Garden), depict scenes and places similar to those that appear in the etchings, or even identical as in the Mountain Moods series.

Ten or so watercolors by Burr can be seen in the Denver Public Library; but the majority — including some that were formerly in public galleries — are now in private hands. I have found the following reproductions, the first, fourth, eighth, and tenth in color:

Azaleas, undated brochure of The Park Floral Co., Denver

Clouds over Colorado Plains, in *Art in America,* XXXIV (Apr. 1946)

Como from Varenna, ibid.

Enchanted Mesa, Archer, *Sonnets to the Southwest* (1930); *Arizona Highways,* XV (June 1939)

Evening near Kremmling, Colorado, in *Art in America,* loc. cit.

In the Gore Cañon, in *The Denver Post,* Dec. 4, 1907.

The Home of Edward [sic] *Stewart White,* ibid.

Lake City, Colorado, Harmsen, *Harmsen's Western Americana* (1971).

A Santa Barbara Garden, in *The Denver Post,* Jan. 11, 1909.

Spring in the Foothills, Morse, *George Elbert Burr, Etcher of the American West* (1967)

Woodland Scene, in *Cameron, Missouri, Centennial* (1955). Untitled; made before Burr left Cameron.

Burr did not always give titles to his paintings. The following representative list[3] contains some actual titles, but many that are derived from exhibition catalogues, newspapers and periodicals, library and museum lists, and public and private collections, must be considered more or less descriptive. In many cases a single item actually represents several paintings done in the same locality.

After the Storm, Arizona	*Capri from Sorrento*
Aigle [Switzerland]	*The Cherwell, Oxford*
Autumn	*Chillon*
Autumn, Rain at Sion, in Rhône Valley	*Church in Stratford*
Autumn, Sion, Switzerland	*Clouds over Colorado Plains*
Azaleas	*Coast near Nevin* [North Wales]
Baveno, Lake Maggiore	*Como from Varenna*
A Bit of Lake Lugano	*A Convent Garden*
Brunnen [Switzerland]	*Cottage near Ross* [Wales]
Byers, Colorado	*Cucharas Valley, Colorado*
Cabin in the Rockies	*Desert Cloud and Butte*
A Canal, Venice	*Desert Clouds*
Capri from Mainland, Dawn	*Desert Moonlight*

---

[3] Most of these seem to be watercolors made before Burr moved to Phoenix in 1924. Additional titles are difficult to trace since his paintings, for the most part acquired promptly by eager buyers and now scattered from coast to coast, received, as time went on, little or no publicity. It is hoped that much information now wanting will be supplied by present owners.

Desert Shower
Desert Shower and Rainbow
Desert Sunrise
Desert Sunset
Desolation
Devil's Bridge, Lucca [Italy]
Ely Cathedral [England]
Enchanted Mesa [New Mexico]
Entrance to a Garden, Bordighera,
    Italy
Estes Park, Colorado
Evening
Evening Clouds, Arizona
Evening from Marshall Pass
    [Colorado]
Evening Glow, Kremmling
Evening near Kremmling, Colorado
Evening near Monte Carlo
Evening, near Rome
Fairy Glen, Bettws-y-coed, North
    Wales
Florence from Monte Oliveto
Florence from San Miniato
Flüelen, Dawn
Flüelen, Lake Lucerne
From Brunnen, Lake Lucerne
From Deer Mountain, Estes Park
From Montreux, Lake Geneva
From North Denver
From Vevay, Lake Geneva
A Garden, Bordighera [Italy]
Gate of San Paolo, Rome
Gathering Storm, Brunnen, Lake
    Lucerne
Gathering Storm, Santa Barbara
A Glimpse of the Grand Canyon
Harlech Castle [North Wales]
Harlech Sands
High Street, Oxford, A Rainy Day
The Home of Edward [sic] *Stewart*
    White [probably the author
    Stewart Edward White, then
    living in Santa Barbara]
Home of the Winds
Hot Day near Goffs [California]
Hy Brasail, or The Isle of the Blest
    [mythical island in n. Atlantic,
    variously spelled (Brazi, Brazil,
    Bresil, etc.)]
Iffley Mill
In a Village, near Mentone [Italy]
In the Gore Cañon, Colorado
James Peak, Evening [Colorado]

The Jungfrau
Lake City, Colorado
Lake Como
Lake Geneva, Dawn
Lake Lucerne, from Brunnen
Lake Lucerne from Rigi Path, Morning
Lake Lucerne from Weggis, Morning
Lake Thun [Switzerland]
Lausanne
Marshall Pass, Colorado
Mentone [Italy]
Mer-de-Glace, Chamonix
Mesa
Morning
Morning, Sion [Switzerland]
Mt. Blanc
Mt. Blanc, Morning
Mt. Byers, Colorado, Sunrise
Mt. Byers, Morning
Mt. Etna from Taormina
Mt. Evans and "Captain Rock"
        from Evans Ranch
Mt. Evans, Colorado
Mt. Evans from Boutwell Cabin
Mt. Evans, Sunrise
Mouth of the Arno
My Castle in Spain
Near Bettws-y-coed, N. Wales
Near Kingman, Arizona
Near Mentone [Italy]
Near Ouray, Colorado
Near Telluride, Colorado
Needles Mountains, Colorado River
Oak Trees, Santa Barbara
October Day, Venice
Old Bridge on the Moselle [Coblenz]
Old Bridge, Rapallo [Italy]
Old Bridge, Venice
Old Cedar, New Mexico
Old Church, Capri
An Old Church, Taormina, Sicily
Old Mill
Old Mill, Chester, England
Old Olive, Mentone [Italy]
Olive Trees, Genoa
A Palace
Pathway in Garden of Miss Dreer,
    Santa Barbara
The Pergola, Lake Lugano
Pikes Peak
Pikes Peak from Manitou
The Plain, Evening [Colorado]
Plains from the Shack [Colorado]

Plains near Denver
Rain over the Plains
Rain, San Francisco Mountains,
Arizona
Rainy Afternoon, High Street, Oxford
The Range at Sunset [Colorado]
Rapallo, Italy
The Rheinfels, St. Goar, on Rhine
The Rhine at Caub
The Rhine at Oberwesel
Rigi, Morning, Lake Lucerne
The Road to Grand Pré, Nova Scotia
Rome from the Campagna, Evening
Rome from Tivoli
Rome, Morning in the Campagna
San Giorgio, Venice
San Michele, Venice
A Santa Barbara Garden
Santa Maria della Salute, Venice (see
Fig. 57)
Sentinel Pine
Sicily
Sierre [Switzerland]
Sion, Switzerland, Dawn
Sketch, Lake Geneva
Snow and Cloud
Snowdon [North Wales]
S.E. from Foothills Cabin
Spanish Peaks, Autumn
Spanish Peaks, Colorado
Spanish Peaks from La Veta, Colo-
rado, Springtime
Spanish Peaks from near Trinidad
Spring Flowers and La Veta Moun-
tain, Colorado
Spring in the Alps
Spring in the Foothills
Springtime, Bordighera [Italy]
Springtime, Lake Lugano

Stepping Stones, Bettws-y-coed
[North Wales]
Storm near Timberline
Street in Gandria [Italy]
Street in Siena [Italy]
Street in Taormina [Sicily]
Street Scene, Amalfi [Italy]
Summer Shower
Summer Shower from Our Cabin
[Colorado]
Sunset in the San Juan Mountains,
Colorado
Sunset, Nevin [North Wales]
Sunset, Ross Churchyard, Wales
Sustenthal [Switzerland]
Swiss Chalet, Interlaken
Temple at Paestum [Italy]
Temple of Castor & Pollux, Girgenti
[Sicily]
Temple of Ceres, Paestum
The Thunderhead
Tree and Brook
Twilight in Arizona
A Valley in North Wales
Valley of the Wye, North Wales
Venetian Fishing Boats
Venice
Ventimiglia [Italy]
View from Dickville Notch, N.H.
View of the Cappuccini, Amalfi
Villeneuve, Lake Geneva
Washing Place, Siena [Italy]
Waves at La Jolla, California
Whirlwinds
A Window, Taormina [Sicily]
Windsor Castle, Morning
Windswept Spruces
Woodland Scene

Glossary and Key to Abbreviations

Aquatint. A mottled, granular effect made by dusting certain areas of the plate with a porous *ground* (usually powdered resin), which allows only partial corrosion of the plate where the acid eats through the interstices between the grains. Aquatint is used to produce tonal areas in a rich range of gradations that is controlled by the number of successive immersions in the acid bath. It is usually combined with linear effects of pure *etching,* or with *soft ground, drypoint,* etc. A similar effect is produced by lightly pressing sandpaper into ordinary hard ground.

Artist's Proof. See *Proof.*

Color Etching (Burr's method; see also Chapter III). When the copper plate is finished and ready for printing, it is painted with oil colors (instead of ink) and a single impression is made on damped paper. The entire process of painting must be repeated for each new impression.

Copy. As used here, an original etching, drypoint, etc., in any state including trial proofs.

Del. et Imp. For Latin *delineavit et impressit;* following the artist's name, "He drew and printed [it]."

Drypoint. Direct etching on copper without the line being bit by acid. The plate is scratched by a sharp tool (stronger than the etching needle), which is drawn, unlike the engraver's burin, *toward* the user. The amount of pressure used determines the depth and thickness of the line, which, when printed, often appears to stand out in relief. The tool raises a slight burr; this retains the ink and produces a line that gives tones from gray to a velvety black depending

173

upon the amount of scraping applied to the furrows. Repeated printing and wiping wear down the burr, so that only a limited number of proofs can be struck unless the plate is faced with a thin coating of steel (see Chapter VI, item #293). Drypoint lines are sometimes added to etched plates for additional richness and variety.

Edition.   The total run of etchings pulled from final state of the copper plate.

Engraved Line.   A line incised in the plate with a sharp-pointed burin or graver, which has a handle that rests against the palm of the hand. As opposed to *drypoint*, the tool is pushed *forward* by the user, and the slight burr that is raised is removed with a scraper.

Etching.   (1) In its commonest form, an intaglio process that produces, by chemical action, incised lines on the surface of a polished plate, usually of copper. The lines are not cut by a tool directly into the metal; the plate is coated with a thin layer of resinous *ground* on which the artist draws his sketch with a needle or other suitable sharp instrument. Through these openings in the ground, the acid bites into the plate, the number of immersions in the acid bath determining the quality and thickness of the lines. These are often reinforced by additional lines cut into the metal by hand (see *Drypoint; Engraved Line*). Still other etching techniques are described under *Aquatint, Color Etching, Mezzotint,* and *Soft Ground.* (2) An impression on paper taken in ink (or in oils) from an etched plate, representing either pure etching, one of the processes named above, or combinations of these.

Giant Cactus.   A common name for the saguaro cactus.

Ground.   (1) In pure etching, a varnish-like mixture (beeswax, bitumen, and resin) laid over the polished plate as an acid-resistant coating. Through this the artist draws his sketch with the etching needle, thus exposing the metal beneath to eventual biting by the acid. Burr is said to have made his own ground to use on location, specially adapted to the heat of the western deserts. (2) In *soft ground,* the ground is mixed with an adhesive such as tallow. (3) In *aquatint,* a specially prepared powdered ground is dusted over portions of the plate.

Impression.   An original etching, drypoint, etc., including any trial proof. Burr printed all his own etchings.

In Color.   See *Color Etching.*

Limber Pine.   *Pinus flexilis,* found in the Rocky Mountains at timber line, often storm-battered and distorted, has a dense crown and remarkably flexible branches.

Mezzotint.   Like *drypoint,* mezzotint utilizes raised burrs. The entire polished plate is first roughened by pricks of the *roulette* or by short, crisscross lines made with the *rocker.* Thus prepared, it would, when inked, print a solid black. The design is made by burnishing and scraping certain areas to obtain intermediate tones. A somewhat similar diffused effect is achieved by pressing sandpaper onto the plate — or (an easier procedure) a bit of woven cloth onto the ground itself. (The sandpaper technique is described in Chapter VI under #293.) Burr (like most modern etchers) found the mezzotint process to be arduous and uncongenial except as an auxiliary process — it is probably the least spontaneous method of preparing the plate for printing; see his remark under #68 *Arizona Clouds* [no. 1].

Monogram. Burr's initials combined within a minute square etched on the plate. Burr sometimes designated a superior impression by adding, in the lower margin, a hand-written, circled monogram.

NYPL. The New York Public Library (the Print Room).

Park. In Colorado, a level, open area surrounded by mountains or forests.

Plate. Burr always used a plate of copper, the metal favored by most etchers.

Plate Mark. The slight impression left on the damped paper by the plate as it is run through the press. It is more conspicuous on some kinds of paper than on others. If a plate mark is cut away, the "clipped" etching is thereby reduced substantially in value.

Print. As used here, an original etching, drypoint, soft ground, etc., which has been, as the term applies, printed or impressed. All etchings are prints; not all prints are etchings.

Proof. Burr applied the term "proof" or "final proof" indiscriminately to what is commonly called "artist's proof" — the final *trial proof* pulled from the plate before beginning the run. These impressions represent the ultimate in brilliance and perfection; they are usually reserved for the artist's personal use, and, in Burr's case, are always signed. Sometimes (see, for example, #345) he uses "proof" in the sense of "trial proof." See also *Trial Proof.*

Remarque. An occasional sketch, either simple or intricate, made by an artist on one or more margins of his plate, serving to test his tools or method, to identify a particular proof or state, or merely to satisfy a whim. Common during the nineteenth century, remarques are rarely found today. Three etched by Burr are described in Chapter VI under #19 *Study of Pines* [no. 5], #26 *Brook in Snow*, and #264 *Fish Creek, Apache Trail, Arizona* (see Fig. 40).

Rocker or Cradle. A small, curved, spade-like blade cut with fifty or more fine teeth to the inch, in various configurations. Held by its handle at right angles to the plate, it imparts indentations and burrs as it is rocked over the surface of the copper. The *roulette* is also used for roughing a plate.

Roulette. A tool fitted with a small, revolving wheel for making dots or various lined indentations through the ground, or, in mezzotint, directly onto the plate to give a granulated surface. Its use declined somewhat after the invention of the *rocker.*

Soft Ground. The quickest and most spontaneous method of preparing an etched plate. A drawing is made with a pencil or stylus on a sheet of tissue or tracing paper laid over a plate coated with a soft, adhesive *ground.* The pressure of the instrument causes the ground to adhere to the paper, leaving on the plate soft, broken lines that give the effect, after immersion in the acid bath, of pencil or crayon lines. Soft ground is often used with *aquatint* to give a pleasing effect to masses and textures.

State. When a plate has been readied for printing, a proof printed from it will show the first state of that plate. Any alterations to the plate will constitute a new state.

Stone Pine. *Pinus pinea*, a tree with a broad, umbrella-shaped head, common in the Mediterranean area.

Trial Proof. While etching a plate, the artist now and then inks it and pulls an impression in order to study the progress of his work. He may pull only a few in each *state,* or as many as a dozen as he experiments with various inks, stopping-out varnish, the acid bath, techniques, paper, etc. These working proofs are not considered a part of the *edition.* Ideally they should be marked with the trial-proof number and state number, data of great importance to collectors; but Burr rarely bothered to write more than the notation "trial proof." A comparison of his trial proofs shows that changes made on the plate are often insignificant; but there are exceptions where large areas are altered, the plate cut to a different size, etc. Although these proofs, like the finished etchings, are usually signed in pencil on the lower left margin, a few unsigned copies will doubtless be discovered — all probably printed by him, since he and his wife destroyed all but a very few of his plates. See also *Proof.*

Selected Bibliography

NOTE: *Letters cited in the text are not included. Their locations, following names of addressees, are: Curator of Prints, Brooklyn Museum (Brooklyn Mus.); Jaques; Tolman (Smithsonian Inst.); Jones; Rutherford; Spalding (Denver Pub. Lib.); Macbeth Gallery (Archives of Amer. Art, microfilm); Mechlin (Phila. Mus. of Art; Archives of Amer. Art, microfilm); Weitenkampf (NYPL).*

ALLHUSEN, E. L. *George Elbert Burr, Etcher.* [Denver, c. 1928.] [Reprinted from *The Studio* (London).]

————. "George Elbert Burr's Etchings of the Desert." *The Studio* (London), LXXXIII (Mar. 15, 1922), 136–144.

"American Deserts Etched." *International Studio*, LXXVIII (Oct. 1923), 57–64.

American Prints in the Library of Congress. A Catalog of the Collection, comp. Karen F. Beall et al. Baltimore: Johns Hopkins Press, [1970].

ARCHER, LOU ELLA. *Sonnets to the Southwest.* [Phoenix: Privately Printed, 1930.]

"Arizona Sketch Book: George Elbert Burr." *Arizona Highways*, XV (Aug. 1939), [19–26]. [Text by Carolann Smurthwaite.]

ARMS, JOHN TAYLOR. *Handbook of Print Making and Print Makers.* New York: Macmillan, 1934.

[BISHOP, HEBER REGINALD]. *The Bishop Collection. Investigations and Studies in Jade.* 2 vols. New York: Privately Printed, 1906. [See also entry New York National Academy of Design.]

————. *De Luxe Catalogue. The Art Collection Formed by the Late Heber R. Bishop*, ed. Thomas E. Kirby. New York: J. J. Little, 1906. [Executors' catalogue for public sale (10 afternoons, 3 evenings) conducted by Amer. Art Assoc. Illustrations by Burr.]

[Bronson, Charles Cook, comp.]. *The Bronson Book. Accounts of the Establishment and Early Settlement of the Connecticut Western Reserve as Written and Collected from the Writings of Early Pioneers by Charles Cook Bronson [1804–1886].* [Stow, O.: Stow Public Library, 1954.]

Bulletin of the New York Public Library, XL (Mar. 1936), 282. [Comments on recently acquired collection of 287 Burr etchings.]

Cameron, Missouri, Centennial, 1855–1955. [Cameron, 1955.] [Contains (p. [44]) small reproduction of Burr watercolor and photo of the artist.]

"Catalogue Raisonné of the Etchings of George Elbert Burr." *The Print Connoisseur,* III (Jan. 1923), 81–86.

Cheney, Sheldon. "Notable Western Etchers." *Sunset,* XXI (Dec. 1908), 737–744.

"59 Burr Etchings Given to Boston Museum." *The Art Digest,* IV (May 1, 1930), 21.

Fine Prints of the Year. London & New York, 1923–.

Fisher, Theo[dore] Merrill. "George Elbert Burr." *The American Magazine of Art,* X (Feb. 1919), 124–129.

Frank, John P. *The Phoenix Art Museum; a History.* Phoenix: John P. Frank, 1969.

Frank Leslie's Illustrated Newspaper, Dec. 28, 1889–Jan. 30, 1892.

"George Burr Dies." *The Art Digest,* XIV (Dec. 1, 1939), 25.

George Elbert Burr. American Etchers series, Vol. VII. New York: The Crafton Collection; London: P. & D. Colnaghi, [1930]. [Contains 5-page introduction by Arthur Millier; catalogue of Burr's etchings (Nos. 1–314); 12 full-page reproductions. Seventy-five additional copies, printed on hand-made paper and containing an original etching signed by Burr, were sold through advance subscription.]

Green, Frank A. [Biographical and historical data of Stow, Ohio, as copied from the record book of Frank A. Green, sexton of Stow Cemetery, from Nov. 1, 1924.] MS in Stow Public Library.

Harmsen, Dorothy. *Harmsen's Western Americana.* Flagstaff: Northland Press, 1971.

Laver, James. *A History of British and American Etching.* London: Ernest Benn, 1929.

McCauley, Lena M. *George Elbert Burr's Etchings of the Desert (New Mexico – Arizona – California).* [Denver: Privately Printed, c. 1921.]

————. *George Elbert Burr, Painter-Etcher.* N.p.: Privately Printed, 1923.

————. "Mr. Burr's Etchings of National Import." *The Chicago Evening Post,* Aug. 16, 1921, sect. "News of the Art World."

M[echlin], L[eila]. "New Plates by George Elbert Burr." *The American Magazine of Art,* XX (June 1929), 328–334.

Morse, A[lbert] Reynolds. "George Elbert Burr and the Western Landscape." *Art in America,* XXXIV (Apr. 1946), 73–90.

————. *George Elbert Burr, Etcher of the American West, 1859–1939.* N.p.: Privately Printed for the Reynolds Morse Foundation and the Denver Public Library, 1967.

————. "The Life and Works of George Elbert Burr, Pioneer Etcher of the Great Southwest (1859–1939)." 1947. MS in Denver Public Library (Special Collections Room).

Muir, John, ed. *Picturesque California: The Rocky Mountains and the Pacific Slope.* 2 vols. New York & San Francisco: J. Dewing, 1888.

"National Museum [Washington, D.C.] Presents Desert Prints." *The Art Digest,* IV (mid-Jan. 1930), 21.

[New York National Academy of Design]. *Loan Exhibition. 1893. Descriptive Catalogue of Works in Bronze and Iron Loaned from the Collection of Mr. Heber R. Bishop.* New York: National Academy of Design, [1893]. [Illustrations by Burr.]

NOYES, RUSSELL. *Wordsworth and the Art of Landscape.* Indiana University Humanities Series No. 65. Bloomington, Ind., 1968.

Palette & Bench, II (May 1910), 187. [Editorial on George Senseney and the art of color etching.]

PERRIN, WILLIAM HENRY, ed. *History of Summit County, with an Outline Sketch of Ohio.* Chicago: Baskin & Battey, 1881.

POWELL, EDITH WILLIAMS. "George Elmer [sic] Burr; an Etcher of the Desert." *The Print Connoisseur,* I (June 1921), 311–321.

SENSENEY, GEORGE E. "Etching in Color." *Palette & Bench,* II (May 1910), 192–194.

SIMMONS, WILL. "The Etchings of George Elbert Burr." *Prints,* III (Nov. 1932), 1–9.

_____. "George Elbert Burr, Etcher of the American Desert." *The Print Connoisseur,* X (Oct. 1930), 256–281.

SMURTHWAITE, CAROLANN. "An Arizonian Tribute to a Great Etcher." *The Arizonian* (Scottsdale, Ariz.), XV (Sept. 22, 1967), 5.

_____. "George Elbert Burr." *Arizona Highways,* XX (June 1944), [16–25].

_____. See entry "Arizona Sketch Book: George Elbert Burr."

"26 Museums Own 700 Works by Burr, Etcher." *The Art Digest,* VI (June 1, 1932), 16.

WARD, MORRIS R. "The Etchings of George Elbert Burr." *The International Studio,* LIV (Nov. 1914), 11–14.

WHITELEY, PHILIP W. "George Elbert Burr: Pioneer Etcher of the Southwest." *The Denver Westerners Monthly Roundup,* XVIII (June 1962), 5–9.

_____. "George Elbert Burr, Pioneer Etcher of the Southwest." The Westerners. Denver Posse. *Brand Book; Containing . . . Original Papers Relating to Western and Rocky Mountain History.* Denver: The Westerners, 1963. [An expansion of the preceding item.]

Year Book of American Etching. New York: John Lane et al., 1914–.